The Voter's Guide to Election Polls

The Voter's Guide
to Election Polls

Michael W. Traugott
University of Michigan

and

Paul J. Lavrakas
Northwestern University

CHATHAM HOUSE PUBLISHERS, INC.
CHATHAM, NEW JERSEY

The Voter's Guide to Election Polls

Chatham House Publishers, Inc.
Box One, Chatham, New Jersey, 07928

Copyright © 1996 by Chatham House Publishers, Inc.

Publisher: Edward Artinian
Production supervisor: Katharine F. Miller
Cover design: Lawrence Ratzkin
Composition: Bang, Motley, Olufsen
Printing and binding: R.R. Donnelley & Sons Company

Library of Congress Cataloging-in-Publication Data

Traugott, Michael W.
    The voter's guide to election polls / Michael W. Traugott and
Paul J. Lavrakas.
        p.   cm.
    Includes bibliographical references (p.   ) and index.
    ISBN 1-56643-046-1 (pbk.)
    1. Public opinion—United States.   2. Public opinion polls.
    3. Election forecasting—United States. 4. Press and poli-
    tics—United States. I. Lavrakas, Paul J. II. Title.
HN90.P8T73   1996
303.3'8'0973—dc20   96-10014
                                                               CIP

Manufactured in the United States of America
        10   9   8   7   6   5   4   3   2   1

To our parents,
Fritz and Lucia
John and Catherine
For their love and support

CONTENTS

INTRODUCTION

Contemporary American politics is awash in polling data. Everywhere a citizen turns, polls are reporting the standing of the candidates. There is a constant stream of "horserace" news stories describing candidates' behavior as strategic acts prompted by the campaign's latest polls. And there are frequent expressions of concern about the impact of polls on the public, such as election-night projections based on exit polls that are perceived to have an effect on turnout on the West Coast, where the voters still have time to cast their ballots.

After the 1996 Iowa caucuses, millionaire Steve Forbes was criticized by his Republican opponents and many in the media for spending more than $400 per vote he received. But little of the same kind of complaint was directed at a new kind of poll-based programming effort by PBS, which produced a short series of programs based on a "deliberative poll" involving 459 people who spent a weekend in Austin, Texas—at a total cost of about $10,000 per respondent. The cost of engaging in political discourse is obviously not a good measure of the quality of a democracy.

The 1996 presidential campaign has seen instances wherein one form of pseudo poll, called a "push poll" by candidates and their consultants, was used in attempts to sway supporters and suppress turnout in the early primaries. Forbes, a relative newcomer to presidential politics, and Patrick Buchanan, an older hand, called these "dirty tricks"; other, more experienced Republican candidates described them as a standard campaign tool.

Is the average citizen supposed to treat all these "polls" as equivalent and accept their "findings" with alacrity? Or is it possible to acquire a reasonable amount of knowledge and information about what polls are and how they are conducted and then apply it in order to distinguish the "good" from the "bad"?

This book was written to help students of politics—those still in school and those who are out in the real world but still striving to increase their understanding of how the process of presidential nomination and selection works—appreciate the use of polls during election campaigns. An equally important goal is to help citizens develop a more critical view of how polls *do* and *don't*, yet *could* and *should*, contribute to a more informed electorate and a better functioning democracy.

Our sense of a need for a book like this came from frequent speaking engagements and presentations about political polling and its link to contemporary journalism. When speaking to students, citizens groups, and alumni gatherings at our respective universities, we learned that people are interested in and concerned about the roles of polling in political campaigns and the news coverage that is based on them. Within our lifetime, news organizations have increasingly moved from being conveyors of this information and to serving as active purveyors of it through their own polling organizations.

Polling, the News Media, and Politics

Elections have a special place in American journalism, for several reasons. One reason is that we live in a democracy, and public opinion has such a central role in the functioning and legitimacy of our government. Elections, and the campaigns leading up to them, are the defining political act in the United States. They represent a point at which most Americans devote more time to thinking about politics and public affairs than normal. The election of public officials with broad public support—and the "mandates" that might be involved—is a critical underpinning of our system of representation.

At the same time, elections make great news. They involve important issues and, eventually, well-known figures. They operate under a system of rules that most citizens are familiar with. They occur on a fixed schedule, involve substantial conflict, and ultimately come to a neat resolution on Election Day with the declaration of winners and losers. Moreover, campaigns are populated by willing sources interested in talking with journalists and having their side of the story presented in the best possible light. For all these reasons, there is a strong symbiotic relationship between journalists and candidates. They rely on each other for success, even though they often seem at odds with each other.

One of their common interests is how the public feels about the campaigns, the issues, and the candidates—what the "public mood" is. In the old days, both candidates and journalists relied on various "experts" for these assessments. They included party leaders, elected officials, and such unobtrusive indicators as the size of crowds that turn out for scheduled events. But the size of a crowd, for example, is an imperfect measure of public opinion because it is often difficult to associate a good measure of valence or affect with sheer numbers of participants, as well as to gauge the intensity of feelings associated with the views that its members hold. For a very long time, what was missing in American politics was a way to produce systematic and reliable measures of public opinion, information that could be used to plan or revise strategy or to contextualize reporting of what the candidates were saying and doing.

While politicians and journalists have always been interested in knowing about public opinion, the extensive application of survey research techniques did not begin until the 1930s, when the "founding fathers," such as George Gallup, Elmo Roper, and Archibald Crossley, began to collect and publish opinion data. From the start, their efforts were possible because of relationships they established with newspapers and magazines. They needed the mass media to serve as outlets for the wide dissemination of their results because their public opinion business was a way of promoting their firms' proprietary work for commercial clients. And these news outlets were always looking for new and timely content.

After World War II, improvements in sampling methods and increasing commercial demand for survey research led to an increase in polling. The candidates themselves turned to public opinion polls as an integral part of their own research efforts, using the information to supplement analyses of historical voting patterns. At the same time, the public dissemination of data rapidly accelerated after the important news organizations in the United States—the networks and major metropolitan daily newspapers—began to collaborate on their own independent data collection. Now the news coverage of presidential campaigns is filled with poll results, both from polls leading up to a primary or general election day and then from exit polls of voters leaving their balloting places. The former data are used to explain and dissect the campaign, and the latter are used to provide poll-based explanations of the "meaning" of the outcome, as well as to project the winners.

News organizations and journalists justified their entry into the polling business because they believed that the use of poll data contributed to their objectivity in producing news about politics. When they purchased results from the Gallup poll, or one of its competitors, they acquired useful content at a reasonable price. Technological shifts that reduced the cost of polling—most notably the penetration of telephones into virtually every American household and the availability of microcomputers that serve as low-cost interviewing devices and data analysis machines—raised the prospect of independent data-collection activities. And news organizations further justified this on the basis of increased editorial control: they could ask *whatever questions* they wanted and put studies into the field *whenever* they wanted if they ran their own polling operations.

These are the technological and business trends that accelerated the production of polling data and their increased use in news making. They explain why we have more polls, but they do not tell us what difference polls make or what impact they have on American political life. These are more subjective issues, but we do have a view on this.

There is a substantial body of literature, growing in size and increasingly compelling in terms of the evidence mustered, that indicates that polls have a substantial impact on the American political process. Poll results have an impact on the vitality and viability of candidacies, affecting who can raise money, organize a field staff, and secure volunteers. News coverage containing poll results has an impact on assessments that citizens make of candidates and how they decide to vote. And polls clearly have an effect on how campaigns are covered, as reporters, editors, and producers use this information to make decisions about who to cover and how to frame the coverage.

We are not opposed to polls and polling; on the contrary, we see election polls in terms of their largely unfulfilled potential. There is plenty of room for them to make a substantial contribution to levels of citizen knowledge and understanding of the political process, including the provision of information about how fellow citizens see the political world in terms of issues and how they respond to candidates and their campaigns.

Unfortunately, these possibilities go largely unrealized because too much campaign reporting is devoted to who is ahead and who is behind—a form of "horserace" coverage to which polls easily lend themselves. Polls are also used to support explanations of campaign strategy and dynamics, rather than focus on the issues that concern voters and their appreciation and understanding of what the candidates have to say about them.

Our hope is that if citizens understand more about how polls are conducted, analyzed, and reported in the media, they will be able to think about other ways in which such information would be useful to them. And on an informed basis, they will be able and want to exert pressure on news organizations to alter some elements of their coverage so they will be more responsive to the informational interests and needs of their readers and viewers.

The Organization of This Book

We faced two fundamental issues in organizing this book: What information should we present? And how should we present it? On the first score, we used our own backgrounds in survey research, mass communication, and political science to select appropriate topics and organize them in a useful way. On the second score, we adopted a question-and-answer format for presenting the information because our dealings with students and other members of the public suggested that there was a thirst for more information about polls—where they come from, how they are used, and with what effect—that was most commonly expressed to us in question form.

On the matter of content, we have organized the book in ten chapters that highlight the major elements surrounding polls and polling in the United States: their history and adoption by news organizations; the basics of data-collection techniques; typical analysis strategies; and, finally, keys to understanding and interpreting poll results based on a critical review of the sources of the data. These are the main areas of interest and concern that people have expressed when we talk with them.

The book begins with an introduction to polls and surveys that provides a broad overview of what they are and where they come from. This set of principles is extended to political polls, and the differences in polls conducted for candidates and media organizations. This first section ends with a general description of how news organizations collect and report election poll data.

In the next section, the four main elements of the design and analysis of polls are discussed. These include sampling procedures, interviewing procedures, and the design of questionnaires. These chapters cover such topics as scientific and unscientific procedures for selecting respondents, and what difference they make. This is followed by a discussion of how interviews take place and the differences between talking to people face-to-face, on the telephone, or using a self-administered questionnaire. Then the content turns to how individual questions are written and how they are combined to form questionnaires. Finally, different elements of analysis are described in a nontechnical way that highlights principles and does not involve any detailed statistical concepts or procedures.

The book concludes with chapters on evaluating polls and a discussion of common problems and complaints about polls—some of which have merit and others of which do not. Based on the concepts of "good" and "bad" practice covered in the preceding chapters, we offer the reader a guide to evaluating polls and poll-based content they might encounter. And we provide a framework for thinking about election polls and the contributions they might make to politics and an informed citizenry.

Within each chapter, the information is presented in a question-and-answer format intended to simplify the presentation and interpretation of important points. In a certain sense, the formulation of these questions was the easiest part of our task. These are the questions that people always ask us, directly or indirectly, depending on their level of prior knowledge and their ability to formulate their interests and concerns in a particular way.

In some cases, we developed a list of key questions and then found we had to develop a list of prior questions whose answers would inform the meaning of and response to the question we started with. Sometimes, the formulation of the answer to a question led to another question and the need to answer it. Finally, we developed answers to each question, first dividing up the questions between us and eventually reviewing each other's responses to the questions. Each answer was prepared with a goal of keeping the length relatively short and the language as simple and direct as possible when dealing with a relatively technical subject. As a further aid to the reader, we have incorporated a glossary to the book containing brief definitions of key concepts. Each chapter has an annotated bibliography to steer the reader to additional discussions of the main topics addressed in that section. And there are appendixes that contain the key provisions of the public disclosure statements of the two main organizations devoted to public opinion research in the United States: the American Association for Public Opinion Research (AAPOR) and the National Council of Public Polls (NCPP).

Concluding Comments

Any project of this scope requires assistance from a number of people. We discussed the concept with several of our colleagues, and we received useful feedback from Eleanor Singer and Warren Mitofsky, a visitor in Ann Arbor in fall 1995. Santa Traugott was a careful reader and editor of early versions. Any errors or problems that remain are of course our own responsibility.

We started this project on a schedule that seemed reasonable to us, especially since we thought we could write quickly. In the end, the complications of producing this first edition and marketing it during a presidential election year were greater than we expected. All through our discussions with potential publishers, Ed Artinian at Chatham House was supportive and encouraging. In the end, he promised miracles in the production phase, and he has fulfilled all his promises.

What Are Polls and Surveys?
And Why Are They Conducted?

A poll or a survey is a method of collecting information from people by asking them questions. Most polls involve a standardized questionnaire, and they usually collect the information from a sample of people rather than the entire population.

People with different interests conduct polls and surveys for many different reasons.

Candidates use polls as an essential part of the intelligence-gathering operation of their campaign. Polls provide a candidate with information about what the voters are thinking and how they are inclined to vote. Many candidates also use poll results to stimulate contributions to their campaigns or to dissuade people from contributing to another candidate.

Media organizations conduct polls to collect information for use in news stories and to form news judgments about what kinds of coverage to provide. A substantial portion of the news derived from polls involves who is ahead and who is behind, and by how much. At the end of the campaign, media organizations use polls to project the winner of the race.

Political scientists and other researchers interested in the dynamics of campaigns and elections use polls to learn about how the candidates behave and how voters respond to campaign stimuli. They try to explain why voters react to candidates in certain ways, but they are usually not interested in projecting the winner of a race.

What is a survey?

A *survey* is a data-collection technique that involves a questionnaire administered to a group of individuals. The *questionnaire* consists of multiple items, or questions, ranging from just a few that take only minutes to complete to several hundred that could take more than an hour to complete. The questionnaire can be administered by an interviewer in a face-to-face setting, on the telephone, in the mail, or by handing it to a respondent to fill out (a self-administered questionnaire).

Questionnaires can include items on a wide variety of topics. The questions can measure behavior ("Did you vote for president in 1992?"), opinions or attitudes ("Do you approve or disapprove of the way Bill Clinton is handling his job as president?"), or the personal characteristics of the respondents ("How old are you?").

The group of individuals interviewed almost always consists of a *sample* selected from a larger population. In order to use the sample to make inferences back to the population, the respondents in the sample must be selected in a scientific way using probability methods.

How does a poll differ from a survey?

In principle, a poll and a survey are the same thing. The term *poll* is usually applied to surveys done by commercial organizations, including media organizations. A poll typically involves a questionnaire containing relatively few questions, and it is conducted across a brief interviewing period (often just a few days). The sample size of a poll usually ranges from 600 to 1,500 respondents.

Surveys are more typically conducted by academic researchers and government researchers. They usually involve much longer questionnaires, and they sometimes involve much larger sample sizes, numbering in the tens of thousands of respondents. The interviewing periods are often much longer, ranging from several weeks to a few months.

How many different kinds of surveys are there?

Depending on the classification criteria, there are several kinds of surveys. One way to classify surveys is by the interviewing technique. Most election polls are conducted on the telephone, but some studies (including exit polls) are conducted using *self-administered questionnaires*. *Face-to-face interviews,* which are the most expensive to conduct, are usually limited to academic and government research projects.

Another way to classify surveys is according to their design, especially in the way that they can be used to measure change. It is common to talk about *cross-sectional surveys, longitudinal studies,* and *panel studies.*

In a *cross-sectional survey,* a single sample of respondents is interviewed once and asked a set of questions. All by themselves, cross-sectional surveys do not measure change. Most polls reported in the media involve this kind of design.

In a *longitudinal design,* the same questions or entire questionnaire is administered over time to a series of independent samples consisting of new respondents each time. The estimates produced by each survey are compared in order to measure gross levels of change in a population.

In a *panel design,* the same respondents are interviewed at more than one point in time, and they are usually asked at least some of the same questions each time. Through a panel design, a researcher can measure change at the individual level by comparing each respondent's answers to the same question at each point in time. This produces a different measure of change than a longitudinal design does.

Are there other ways to obtain people's opinions?

People express their opinions in a variety of ways: through demonstrations and picketing, the kinds and amounts of products they buy, their membership in organizations, or the size of the checks they write to political candidates and special-interest groups. Sales, demonstrations, and memberships are only imperfect indicators of underlying opinions; they do not tell researchers about things like how intensely people hold their opinions or the reasons why they feel the way they do. And they are not reliable or valid indicators of how many people in the population as a whole might hold the same opinions.

The only way to measure opinions in a reliable and valid way is to combine a scientifically drawn and executed sample and a well-designed and executed questionnaire. Information collected in this way is used to draw inferences to the distribution of opinion in the entire population. A probability sample provides the way that inferences can be made back to the population. The questions are used to assess what opinions the public holds, on what basis and with what intensity.

When is a "survey" not a survey?

A scientific poll or survey is used to collect information for aggregated statistical purposes. The data are combined for analysis without concern about who an individual respondent is or what their answers to the questions were.

A "survey" is not a survey when it does not involve a probability sample or it is used to collect information about individuals for some other purpose than research. For example, some things are called surveys that are really just the compilation of statistics into an index. These appear as "surveys" of college quality or business climates. In the former case, they involve compiling information on admission rates, test scores, and the cost of tuition in order to rank schools. In the latter case, they might involve assessment of skill levels in the workforce, tax rates, the cost of utilities, and the like. In neither case is any sample drawn nor is anyone interviewed. In either case, these numbers are combined in some fashion to produce rankings from "best" to "worst."

Sometimes you might receive a solicitation in the mail that contains a questionnaire, often asking a few leading questions and then asking you to join an organization or write a check as part of a fund-raising drive. Typically, the questionnaires that are completed and returned are never tabulated; but the names and addresses of the individuals who returned them are listed and sometimes even sold to other organizations. The purpose of the mailing was to solicit new members or raise money, not to collect data.

In another case, opinions are solicited through questionnaires placed in newspapers or magazines, or by offering an "800" or "900" number for people to call. These data are usually tabulated and presented as news, but they should not be considered surveys because they do not involve scientific samples. The "respondents" are self-selected and unrepresentative of the population as a whole in several ways. These issues are discussed in detail in chapter 10.

Why not just count everyone?

An enumeration, or *census,* of everyone in the population may sometimes be an alternative to a survey, but in the vast majority of cases it will not be as effective as a good survey in producing reliable estimates. A census is usually much more expensive to conduct, and it may be too time-consuming. So surveys provide a cost-effective alternative to censuses.

Many people have the impression that a census is more comprehensive than a survey because information is collected from more people. Every enumeration has problems of *coverage,* however, just as surveys do. For example, the decennial census conducted by the U.S. government has consistently undercounted the population, and this is a cause for concern because the undercount is not random. The census is more likely to miss homeless people, those who are very mobile, and individuals of lower socioeconomic status than other citizens.

Furthermore, if a population is very large, it may take a long time to collect all the data by counting everyone. When a sample is used, information can be collected more quickly. This is an important consideration if the information is time sensitive, like attitudes toward a new candidate entering the race or reactions to a speech that the president just gave.

Why is time such an important factor in media polls?

Time is a critical component in media polls because the *news-*

worthiness of the information collected is related in part to how quickly it can be collected. There is always the risk that new events in the real world can invalidate survey results. When two candidates participate in a debate, a poll is conducted very shortly afterward to measure the electorate's perceptions of the candidates and to find out what the voters learned. But the information has to be reported quickly before one of the candidates makes a major policy speech or begins a new advertising campaign, either of which can change the way that many voters evaluate the candidates.

Who sponsors surveys?

Surveys can be sponsored by many different individuals and groups, and people often use sponsorship to make an initial assessment of how much confidence they should have in the results. If the government or an academic organization sponsors a survey, consumers of the data are inclined to believe that the data are neutral and unbiased. This is also generally true for polls sponsored by media organizations. Poll consumers should be more sensitive to the strategic interests of candidates or special-interest groups who sponsor polls. They should pay careful attention to what kinds of questions they ask or the way in which they report their results.

Who conducts polls?

Polls can be conducted by the same organizations that sponsor them, or the data collection—and even the analysis—can be done under contract. Some polling organizations offer a full range of data-collection services, including designing samples and questionnaires; providing interviewing services, data entry, and statistical analysis; and writing reports. Some firms specialize in just one aspect of surveys, such as sampling or interviewing. Some research projects may involve subcontracting various services to different companies, but the use of computer networks and high-speed data transmission means that the project managers are never very far from their data.

Do polls have an impact on those who are exposed to them?

Polls do have an effect on those who see or hear the results. Sometimes these effects are direct, as people change or adjust their attitudes and opinions based on what they think other people believe. Other times, these effects are indirect, arising because candidates cannot raise enough money to stay in a race, for example, and therefore voters never have a chance to give them serious consideration. The impact of polls on poll consumers is considered in virtually every chapter in this book, and special attention is devoted to this topic in chapters 9 and 10.

References

Backstrom, Charles A., and Gerald Hursh-Cesar. 1981. *Survey Research.* New York: Wiley.
This volume contains a practical guide to the design and conduct of surveys. It has chapters that cover all the main issues associated with planning samples, drawing samples, writing questions and designing questionnaires, conducting interviews, and processing data, including writing reports.

A distinguishing feature of this book is that it is filled with practical examples of how to get various steps accomplished with minimum error. For example, it provides detailed instruction on how to construct a sample frame and draw a sample from it. It also has many practical hints about how to design coding systems for open-end questions. The chapter on data processing contains a very basic introduction to survey data analysis and elementary statistics.

Bogart, Leo. 1985. *Polls and the Awareness of Public Opinion.* New Brunswick, N.J.: Transaction.
This book contains a broad and useful discussion of the way in which the widespread use and acceptance of polls has changed public debate in the United States and the relationship between citizens and the leaders they elect. Bogart was a president of the American Association for Public Opinion Research, and the basic ideas in this volume were part of his presidential address in 1967. Almost twenty years later, they are more fully expounded in a volume that looks at polls, politics, opinion research, and public policy.

Bogart covers important changes in polling methods as a result of basic research and changing technology. Because of his long association with the newspaper business, Bogart focuses on the relationship between polls and journalism, and how they are used to make news as well as supplement standard reportorial techniques.

CONVERSE, JEAN. 1987. *Survey Research in the United States*. Berkeley: University of California Press.
This is the essential history of the development of survey research in the United States. It is based on extensive archival research and extended interviews with many of the central figures in the field. The research underlying this work emphasizes both the individuals and institutions that were critical to the development of the survey-based social and policy research enterprise we know today.

The emphasis is ultimately on the major academic research organizations that developed after World War II: the Bureau of Applied Social Research at Columbia; the National Opinion Research Center at the University of Chicago; and the Survey Research Center, now located within the Institute for Social Research at the University of Michigan.

In order to get to that point, however, Converse has to trace the path through the commercial survey research firms that developed before and during the war and in the period just after, including the stories of their leaders: George Gallup, Archibald Crossley, and Elmo Roper.

FINK, ARLENE, ED. 1995. *The Survey Kit*. Newbury Park, Calif.: Sage.
This nine-volume paperback series will introduce readers to everything they ever wanted to know about survey research. Separate volumes cover topics that range from a general introduction to how to ask questions, how to conduct mail and self-administered surveys, how to conduct interviews by telephone and in person, how to design surveys, how to sample, how to measure survey reliability and validity, how to analyze survey data, and how to report on surveys. Fink is the author of six of the volumes; other authors include Linda Borque and Eve Fielder (self-administered surveys), James Frey and Sabine Oishi (telephone and in-person surveys), and Mark Litwin (reliability and validity). Each volume is brief but comprehensive, and the entire package would cover an introduction to all the important issues.

FOWLER, FLOYD J., JR. 1993. *Survey Research Methods*. 2d ed. Newbury Park, Calif.: Sage.
This best-selling brief text is part of a series on Applied Social Research Methods. It is highly readable as a "first book" on survey research and re-

quires no real statistical sophistication in order to follow or benefit from its instruction. The book takes a broad approach to various aspects of survey research instead of going into depth on any single one. It includes sections on sampling, nonresponse, modes of survey data collection, questionnaire design, and preparing data for analysis. Ethical issues in survey research are also discussed.

A unifying theme throughout the book is Fowler's use of the *total survey design* method, sometimes called the *total survey error* perspective. This approach helps the reader understand the real cost tradeoffs that survey researchers face when allocating fixed budgets to achieve the best possible product. For example, one can spend a large proportion of a budget on questionnaire development only to have the survey's validity undermined by inadequate attention to nonresponse. The book provides the novice with a good guide to what might be considered minimum standards toward which to strive for each of the different parts of a survey.

SINGER, ELEANOR, AND STANLEY PRESSER, EDS. 1989. *Survey Research Methods: A Reader.* Chicago: University of Chicago Press.
This edited volume consists of some of the best articles on survey methodology that have appeared in *Public Opinion Quarterly*, the journal of the American Association for Public Opinion Research. Singer and Presser, in addition to being accomplished survey methodologists, have also been editors of the journal.

The volume contains twenty-nine former journal articles, organized into five sections: the Sample: Coverage and Cooperation; the Questionnaire; Mode of Administration; the Interviewer; and Validation. Each section begins with a brief introduction that frames the main issues, discusses the articles, and describes the relationship between them.

The section on sampling, consisting of six chapters, is as much about problems of nonresponse and bias as it is about fundamental design issues. The section on the questionnaire, consisting of eight chapters, focuses primarily on issues of question wording and scaling of attitudes. The section on mode, consisting of four chapters, addresses issues of differences between telephone and face-to-face interviewing, as well as differences in results produced by different survey organizations, known as *house effects.* The section on the interviewer consists of four chapters, and it focuses on the relationship between interviewer and respondent characteristics and how they can affect responses, as well as training and monitoring of ongoing work. The final section contains seven chapters and presents results from studies that sought to compare survey reports with other indicators of the same behaviors or attitudes.

2

WHAT ARE ELECTION POLLS?
HOW ARE THEY CONDUCTED?

For many citizens, the basic concepts of polling are a mystery. Actually most polls involve only a limited number of techniques. Election polls are just a special use of survey research techniques, employing procedures developed and refined over most of the twentieth century.

Polls begin with the selection of a sample of people to be interviewed, who are called the *respondents*. They must be selected in a scientific way so that they accurately reflect the population they are supposed to represent. In that case, their attitudes and opinions will reflect those of the entire population. The respondents are asked a series of questions in a standardized form, called a *questionnaire*. Most contemporary election polling is conducted on the telephone, although sometimes interviews are conducted face-to-face in people's homes or as they leave their balloting place. The answers to the survey questions are tabulated using computers, and the results can be presented in a variety of ways.

An election poll is a survey conducted on topics related to the campaign or conducted during the main campaign period. Some election polls are conducted for candidates to help them develop strategy and organize their campaign. Others are conducted for media organizations to help them produce news stories. Still others are conducted by political scientists or other social researchers in order to understand how campaigns work and to explain the impact of events and news coverage of them on the voters.

The content of election polls is obviously related to politics —asking respondents about the candidates and issues in the campaign. Most election polls are conducted during the campaign period leading up to Election Day; they are called *preelection polls*. Some polls are conducted on Election Day with voters who are leaving the places where they cast their ballots; these are called *exit polls*. The two kinds of polls share many common characteristics, and each has some unique ones. These similarities and differences are discussed in detail in the answers to the commonly asked questions that follow.

What is an election poll?

The term *election poll* refers to a variety of survey types. Some are conducted for media organizations and are designed to produce content for the news. They are different from market research studies used to understand audience characteristics or to indicate what readers or viewers think about the news coverage of the campaign, for example.

Political consultants conduct another kind of election poll. They do these studies for candidates in order to provide strategic information or feedback to the campaign about how successful their strategy has been. Both kinds of election polls are distinct from election surveys conducted by university-based researchers for analysis of the attitudes and behavior of the electorate.

Some election polls are conducted early in the campaign, when members of the electorate have little information about who the candidates are or what their issue stands are. Other election polls are conducted late in the campaign, just before Election Day, to provide estimates or projections of the outcome of the election. And still other election polls are conducted on Election Day itself, among voters leaving their balloting places, in order to provide projections of results and analysis of voting trends for the news media.

Campaign polls employ different questions asked of different samples. Sometimes the candidate wants to know about voter reaction to hypothetical scenarios in the campaign. Sometimes campaign polls are conducted only among people who describe themselves as "undecided" about their candidate preference. At other times, candidates sponsor polls to demonstrate their popular support so they can increase their fund raising, especially in the primaries. Campaign polls usually have very short interviewing periods, sometimes involving only one or two days of interviewing.

University-based surveys of the electorate usually have the lengthiest questionnaires, often involving interviews that take an hour or more. Their samples may be larger, and the field periods may extend across several weeks. In many cases these surveys are conducted after the election. They provide information for detailed analysis of the electorate but not much content that is newsworthy.

How many kinds of election polls are there?

There are several distinct kinds of election polls. They differ in their purpose, their methodologies, and their timing. Early in the campaign, assessments are made of the voters' own issue positions and their knowledge about the candidates. The relative standing of the candidates is evaluated through "trial heats." These polls are usually conducted with samples of adults eighteen years of age or older or samples of registered voters.

As Election Day approaches, the samples employed in election polls switch to "likely voters," or those who are most likely to go to vote on Election Day. Some media organizations conduct interviews every day with small samples of such voters and then aggregate the data for several successive days. These "tracking polls" focus on who is ahead and behind and how these preferences change across relatively brief periods of time in response to campaign events. Both preelection and tracking polls are usually conducted on the telephone.

On Election Day itself, face-to-face interviews are conducted with voters leaving the balloting locations in their neighborhoods in scientifically selected samples of precincts. These "exit polls" are analyzed to produce estimates by early evening of who is going to win each race; they also provide data for analysis of the factors that led voters to support one candidate over another.

How do media organizations use preelection polls?

News organizations use preelection polls to explore the important issues in the campaign and to explain the dynamics of the campaign and how popular support for the candidates crystallizes or shifts as Election Day approaches. In these ways, preelection polls provide substantial content for preelection news coverage. While the range of analytical possibilities is great, most poll-based reporting focuses on who is ahead or behind. Poll results support the media's natural tendency to engage in "horserace journalism," which focuses on the relative standing of the candidates and how it changes across the campaign. Both print and broadcast media use these kinds of polls.

Exit polls are used to project the outcome of races on election night. Since this is a story best suited to broadcast coverage, television networks and radio stations are most likely to make immediate use of these results. Newspapers also pick up these results to support analysis explaining the meaning of the election; but this analysis does not appear until a day or two after the election.

Are there special problems in conducting preelection polls?

All election polls confront three critical problems, although they are more significant for media organizations and candidates, whose work is almost entirely done before Election Day, than they are for social scientists, who usually do most of their analysis after the election is over. One is generating a good estimate of who is going to vote. A second is capturing the volatility that sometimes appears in the electorate. A third is allocating the preferences of those who say they are "undecided" when they are asked for whom they will vote.

While there is a strong scientific and statistical basis for drawing samples and constructing questionnaires, estimating who will go to vote on Election Day is an area where the practitioner's art comes into play. There is no standard, widely accepted way for estimating a person's likelihood of voting. Most polling organizations combine the answers to several questions to estimate the likely electorate, and some methods work better than others.

It is also important to conduct polls as close to Election Day as possible. The use of telephone interviewing techniques helps pollsters to do this. The American electorate has become increasingly volatile, and more voters are deciding later in the campaign how they are going to vote. Current campaign technology allows candidates to organize and target their advertising campaigns right up to Election Day. So interviews take place at least through the weekend preceding Election Day and sometimes right through the Monday night before, if the race is very close.

In the past fifteen years there have been important changes taking place in how and when Americans vote, and this complicates election polling. Some states permit people to vote at various locations for up to three weeks before Election Day, and such states as Minnesota and North Dakota allow people to register on Election Day itself. It is estimated that almost one in four of the votes in the 1992 presidential election were cast using these "early voting" procedures, including absentee ballots. Some states are also using vote-by-mail procedures, as Oregon did in January 1996 to elect a U.S. senator to replace Robert Packwood. These procedures require that pollsters use new techniques for estimating turnout and the partisan division of the vote, and they are likely to produce some problems for them when they project the outcome of races involving these new procedures, until new polling techniques are perfected.

What is the appropriate population to sample for pre-election polls?

Since registration is a minimum requirement for voting, samples for preelection polls should, in principle, account for this condition. Unfortunately, in most jurisdictions there is no list of registered voters that is both accurate and up-to-date *and* contains telephone numbers. So most preelection polls usually begin with a sample of telephone households and then survey respondents within those households are asked to report whether they are registered or not. More details of sampling procedures are covered in chapter 5.

How do polls measure voting intention?

Voting intention is a concept that actually incorporates two different measures. The first is an indication of which candidate someone prefers, and the second is an indication of how likely a person is to go to vote on Election Day. So voting intention is a combination of candidate preference and likelihood of voting for that person.

The first concept is usually measured by a question in the following form:

> *If the election for president were held today and Bill Clinton was the Democratic candidate and Bob Dole was the Republican candidate, whom would you vote for?*

Respondents can indicate which candidate they prefer, that they have not decided yet, or that they do not intend to vote. The results from this question are usually reported for all these categories.

Likelihood of voting is usually measured by evaluating the responses to a series of questions. As noted earlier, a minimum condition for voting in the United States is that you are registered, so this item is common to all likelihood scales. Other important components of likelihood include the respondents' interest in the current campaign, their history of voting in similar elections in the past, and their knowledge about where people in their neighborhood go to vote.

By combining measures of preference and likelihood, pollsters can produce an estimate of the outcome based on the "probable electorate." They can also evaluate whether turnout will have an impact on the outcome—the effects of lower or higher turnout than expected.

How do polls measure candidate support?

Candidate support is measured through a "trial-heat question," as described earlier. In many surveys, this question is often asked in two parts. First, people are asked for whom they are going to vote. Those who express an initial preference for one candidate or another (their core voters) are then asked how strongly they feel about that choice. Those who say they are "undecided" are then asked toward whom they are "leaning."

The strength of support can be analyzed in several ways. One way is to look at each candidate's "committed" support (those who support him or her "strongly"), as well as the ratio between these two groups. Another way is to look at the "leaners" and how they divide among the candidates. In either case, it is important for the pollster to indicate to the poll's consumers which base of support is being analyzed and what the differences are.

A strong commitment to a candidate is also a good indicator of intention to vote. So the "strong supporters" form the core or base electorate. An analyst can investigate the potential impact of turnout on the election by adding in the leaners and seeing whether their preferences are different from those of the core voters.

What happens to people who have not decided yet?

Every time the trial-heat question is asked in a preelection poll, a significant proportion of respondents say they are undecided or refuse to say who their preferred candidate is. The proportion of undecideds declines as Election Day approaches and voters get to know the candidates better. Some interviewing techniques can reduce the number of undecideds by allowing people to complete a "secret ballot."

There are different ways to report data for undecideds. Some organizations report the undecideds as a distinct category; other organizations produce estimates of voter preferences based on the percentage of those who named a candidate or party, omitting the undecideds. In the first case, an organization might say that 50 percent of the sample expressed a preference for Bill Clinton, 41 percent for Bob Dole, and 9 percent were undecided. If the data were repercentagized on the basis of those who stated a preference (91 percent of the sample), the second organization might produce a 55 to 45 percent preference for Clinton over Dole.

Many polling organizations use an allocation method to assign the undecideds to one candidate or the other. Different polling organizations allocate the undecideds in different ways. One is to divide them equally among the two candidates or in proportion to the division of support among those who have already made up their minds. Another way is to allocate them according to party identification, based on the belief that this is the best indicator of how an "undecided" respondent will vote—an "undecided" Democrat will eventually vote for the Democratic candidate, for example. Over the past thirty years, party identification has become a weaker predictor of presidential vote, so this method is not as reliable as it was in the past. One theory even suggests they should be disproportionately allocated to the challenger, in part because they represent people who are reluctant to tell an interviewer that they will vote against an incumbent!

These allocation schemes can make a big difference in the final estimates of an election's outcome. In the 1992 election, the Gallup Organization changed its allocation method; as a result, it severely overestimated support for George Bush and underestimated support for Bill Clinton. There was a much larger error in the final estimate than Gallup had experienced in the past. Because of the 1992 experience, allocation methods in the final preelection polls are likely to receive a lot of attention at the end of the 1996 campaign, from late October on.

What are tracking polls?

At the end of the campaign, some news organizations sponsor *tracking polls* to keep a daily record of who is ahead and who is behind. This tracking of the lead complements the preoccupation with horserace journalism that many news organizations have with reporting who is ahead and who is behind.

Tracking polls use different methodological techniques to produce daily estimates for the last two to four weeks of the campaign. For example, small samples of respondents can be contacted via telephone every day and asked a very brief series of questions. On their own, these daily samples of 100 to 200 interviews are too small to provide precise estimates of candidate support or one candidate's lead over the other. Therefore, pollsters use *rolling averages* of three consecutive days' worth of interviewing to produce these estimates. So interviews conducted on a Monday in October contribute to the production of estimates for three-day periods that cover Saturday-Sunday-*Monday*, Sunday-*Monday*-Tuesday, and *Monday*-Tuesday-Wednesday.

Each of these estimates is then based on 500 to 600 interviews, aggregated across each of these three-day periods. If candidate A was supported by 49 percent of the sample on Saturday (based on 200 interviews), 45 percent of the sample on Sunday (based on another 200 interviews), and 47 percent of the sample on Monday (based on another 200 interviews), the average support for this period, reported on Tuesday, would be 47 percent (based on a total of 600 interviews).

Are there special problems in conducting tracking polls?

Yes there are, because of the nature of the small daily samples and the way interviews are obtained. Tracking polls are essentially one-night surveys, so they do not employ the same rigorous procedures for sampling and respondent selection that many other polls do. Since interviews are conducted on a single day, typically in the evening, there are rarely any attempts made to recontact a telephone household where no one answered the phone the first time. Furthermore, some polling organizations are less rigorous when they do make contact; instead of selecting a respondent randomly within the household, they may take an interview with whoever answers the phone. Both shortcuts can produce flawed samples of respondents. Some research has shown that "first call" respondents are not only more likely to be older and female but also are more likely to be Republican than those who answer the telephone on subsequent attempts to contact them.

How do tracking polls compare to other preelection polls?

This depends on how the other preelection polls were conducted.

At the end of a campaign, all the polls are usually based on samples of "likely" voters rather than registered voters. In the latter case, respondents are screened for registration status, and only those who say they are registered are asked about candidate preference. Research shows that "likely" voters are more affluent and better educated, factors that make them more likely to be Republicans.

Some news organizations are neither careful nor precise about comparing their tracking polls of "likely" voters to other polls based on samples of registered voters. A shift from samples of registered voters to likely voters can mistakenly make it look like a race suddenly got closer; in reality, it was just the samples that changed. For example, there was a period in October 1992 when this happened, and some news organizations reported that the race between Bill Clinton and George Bush was getting tighter. The reduction in the size of Clinton's lead was simply a methodological artifact of changing from one kind of sample or reporting base to another.[1]

Can the publication of tracking-poll results affect whether or how citizens vote?

Researchers generally talk about two different impacts of exposure to election projections. One is called the *bandwagon effect,* and it suggests that some people tend to support a candidate they believe is going to win. The other is called the *underdog effect,* which suggests that some people tend to support the candidate they know is trailing. Voters affected in either of these two ways can learn about the relative standing of the candidates—who's ahead and who's behind—from the horserace journalism practiced by most news organizations nowadays. That type of reporting is buttressed by polls

---

1. These conclusions have been disputed by some polling observers. See Michael Traugott, "A Generally Good Showing, But Much Work Needs to Be Done," *Public Perspective,* November/December 1992, 14–15; and Larry Hugick, Guy Molyneux, and Jim Norman, "The Performance of the Gallup Tracking Poll: The Myth and the Reality," *Public Perspective,* January/February 1993, 12–14.

to produce estimates from the trial heat of which candidate is ahead or behind.

Some research suggests that knowing who is ahead or behind and by how much can affect respondents' answers to survey questions about candidate preferences. These findings were enhanced in a national survey of voters where some of them were given the results of a current Bush-Dukakis poll before they were asked for whom they were going to vote.[2] These data showed that both bandwagon and underdog effects are present simultaneously in the electorate. In this study, the analysis showed that both effects could occur simultaneously, offsetting each other in estimating the outcome of the "real" election.

The existence of underdog and bandwagon effects in elections (as opposed to research studies) is difficult to prove for a variety of reasons. Measurement is difficult, especially if it is based on respondents' self-reports of how they react to published polls. Analysis of data to prove these effects is complicated, especially if it is based only on surveys taken at one point in time and relatively early in the campaign. But results from a number of experiments in which people are told about the results of real or hypothetical polls before they are asked their own preference suggest that bandwagon and underdog effects are present simultaneously in the electorate, among different groups of people.

What is the chance that a preelection poll will produce an incorrect projection of an election outcome?

It is not uncommon for preelection polls to produce estimates of election outcomes that are different from the division of the vote cast on Election Day. There are several explanations for why this

2. Paul J. Lavrakas, Jack K. Holley, and Peter V. Miller, "Public Reactions to Polling News during the 1988 Presidential Election Campaign," in *Polling and Presidential Election Coverage,* ed. Paul J. Lavrakas and Jack K. Holley (Newbury Park, Calif.: Sage, 1991), 151–83.

might happen, ranging from chance to poor methodology. While well-conducted polls are rarely wrong in picking the winner within the margin of sampling error, poor funding and methodological shortcuts explain why others are likely to be.

In any survey, it is possible to draw a "bad" sample that does not represent the population very well. Most survey responses, such as the responses to the trial-heat question, are reported with a margin of error that suggests an "accurate" estimate 95 times out of 100. This means that a poor estimate (inaccurate to the degree of sampling error) is likely to be produced 1 in 20 times. There is little that a researcher can do about this type of "chance" error, but it has to be kept in mind when interpreting any poll results.

Many other sources of error are possible in preelection polls. The most common is an inability to estimate likely voters, or the people who are most likely to go to their balloting places on Election Day. Sometimes the distribution of preferences among all citizens and those who vote is quite different. Therefore, a bad estimate of turnout can be a serious source of error. These issues are discussed in greater detail in chapter 5.

In the past twenty years, there has been increasing volatility in the American electorate, with more people making up their minds about whom to vote for later in the campaign. Therefore, if pollsters stop interviewing too early in the campaign (two weeks before the election rather than the weekend before the election), they can miss late shifts in voter sentiment or the crystallization of support for one or both candidates. Therefore, their estimates of the outcome could be quite far off.

Finally, there are question wording and question order effects on whom people say they will vote for. Using a secret ballot that respondents mark and drop in a box reduces the proportion of undecideds and is a good way of getting at latent support for a candidate. This is especially important if there is a controversial candidate in a race or if one candidate has a characteristic that might make respondents likely to show support when they really do not intend to support that candidate. Research has shown that voters are sometimes reluctant to say they prefer a male candidate over a female candidate, or a white candidate over an African American candidate, especially when the interviewer's race and/or gender is different from the respondent's. These response problems can produce a biased estimate of candidate preference in the electorate, and sometimes they have done so. These issues are discussed in greater detail in chapter 7.

What are exit polls, and what are they used for?

An *exit poll* is a survey based on interviews with voters as they leave (or exit) their balloting locations. To estimate the outcome of an election in a particular constituency, a sample of its precincts is drawn and an interviewer is sent to each one. On a preselected basis, the interviewer intercepts people who have already voted in order to obtain an interview, say every twenty-fifth or thirty-second person who comes out of the voting place. The interviewer usually hands the voter a questionnaire on a clipboard and asks him or her to fill it out, fold it up, and deposit it in a "ballot box."

Election night projections of the outcome of races are based, in large part, on exit polls. Interviewing people as they leave their voting place overcomes a lot of the problem of respondents' misreporting whether they voted or not when they are interviewed on the telephone, for example. These questionnaires are short because people cannot be kept very long from getting to work or getting home. Exit polls are important because information about the voters' demographics and basic attitudinal predispositions provides powerful explanations, to be examined in election postmortems, for why they voted the way they did.

Exit polls provide an invaluable data source for analyzing the meaning of an election, one that is often important to counteract the "spin" that candidates put on it. In 1980, for example, Ronald Reagan's strategists described his defeat of Jimmy Carter as a turn to the right by American voters and an impetus to a conservative legislative agenda for the new Congress. The exit-poll data showed there was no ideological shift among American voters. They were primarily concerned about Carter's inability to influence the economy, and they wanted a new president whom they hoped would do a better job in reducing inflation.

Who conducts the exit polls?

In 1990, the networks and the Associated Press combined their exit polls into a single operation known as Voter Research and Surveys (VRS). Since 1994, further consolidation has taken place and this joint operation is known as the Voter News Service (VNS). All the networks share the same database on election night, although they use their own methods and models to produce their projections of winners. VNS is a cost-saving arrangement that avoids duplication of effort, providing high-quality data at a lower cost than the sum of what all the networks were spending in previous elections. These data are used primarily by the networks on election night, although some national newspapers, such as the *New York Times*, present important exit-poll results in their analysis in the following day or two. Only the *Los Angeles Times* remains as an alternative source for analysis of voting patterns in the electorate.

Are there special problems in conducting exit polls?

Yes there are, because the interviewers have to shoulder a great deal of responsibility, increasing the potential for introducing errors into the data. Left alone at the precinct, the interviewer is responsible for both selecting respondents and conducting interviews. If there are not enough interviewers at a particular voting site, a single interviewer may end up chasing a chosen voter all the way back to his or her car, losing out on time for an interview with the next designated respondent.

As in any kind of poll, differential response rates can produce problems in exit polls. In the 1992 New Hampshire primary, the VRS exit-poll estimate for the Republican race showed a closer outcome than the raw vote eventually did. The data from early in the day produced an evening news broadcast that suggested trouble for President George Bush in his contest with his main rival, Patrick Buchanan. A postmortem analysis of the results from VRS and three other exit polls suggested that Buchanan voters were more likely to participate in exit polls to indicate support for *their* candidate than were Bush voters.[3] So intensity of feelings can sometimes affect participation in exit polls, just as it does in other procedures where simple self-selection is possible.

What is the chance that an exit poll can produce an incorrect projection of an election outcome?

From a researcher's perspective, the chance is relatively high that a poor estimate can be made—perhaps one in 100 or one in 1,000. On a busy general election night, with contests all across the country, exit-poll interviews, used alone, could produce inaccurate estimates in a few races *just by chance alone.*

In the most sophisticated election analysis operations at the networks, the analysts have statistical models to generate their projections. These models use a lot of additional data beyond the exit polls to make their projections, incorporating historical voting data from the sample precincts in which the interviews were taken. This information includes past turnout and the partisan division of the vote. The computer models use this information to evaluate exit-poll results as they become available, looking at whether the turnout is much higher (or lower) than usual and whether the vote is more or less Democratic (or Republican) than in the past.

In less sophisticated operations, there are other potential sources of exit-poll errors. They include poorly trained interviewers, badly worded questions, and even the use of such unorthodox procedures as asking people to indicate out loud for whom they voted, instead of allowing them to mark a questionnaire confidentially.

3. Warren J. Mitofksy, "What Went Wrong with Exit Polling in New Hampshire," *Public Perspective*, March/April 1992, 17.

Do election night broadcasts of projections affect voting?

There is a great deal of public interest in this question, and most Americans believe that the answer is yes. For example, a majority (51 percent) of people interviewed in 1988 felt that network projections made it less likely for people on the West Coast who had not voted to go to their precincts to vote.[4]

For researchers, however, this is a very complicated and difficult question to answer. No studies have proved an unequivocal relationship between election night broadcasts and levels of turnout or margin of vote for a particular candidate. But there is experimental and quasi-experimental evidence suggesting that some people are affected by election night projections. When the outcome of the election is known, some people will have a tendency to stay home rather than go to their local balloting place. And others may be affected by bandwagon and underdog effects.

Are Americans concerned about the effects of election polls?

Ever since the polling business started, surveys have periodically been conducted to find out what citizens know about polling methods and how they feel about the publication or broadcasting of results during election campaigns. For more than twenty years, surveys have been conducted on various aspects of voters' responses to changes in regulation of the polls.

The results show several interesting things. The typical citizen does not know very much about the methodology of polls, certainly not enough to be able to distinguish between surveys that are well done and those that are not. In general, citizens say they are interested in polling information during most of the campaign, and most believe that poll results contribute positively to the campaign coverage.

The major conditional on this is that at the end of the campaign, many voters seem to want to be left alone to make up their

4. Lavrakas, Holley, and Miller, "Public Reactions to Polling News during the 1988 Presidential Election Campaign," 171.

minds in peace. They say they do not want to be bombarded with a torrent of poll data showing who is ahead and who is behind. A special case of this concern is voters who are willing to trade information early on election night about who the winner is for a "quiet period" that would allow voters on the West Coast to cast their ballots without knowing the outcome of the presidential election.

Can the U.S. government regulate how media organizations conduct and disseminate their poll results?

The answer to this question is clearly no under the Constitution. The Supreme Court has consistently found that the First Amendment prohibits any "prior restraint" on the collection and dissemination of news. Therefore, it is unlikely that Congress would pass any law that could survive a court test to eliminate the publication of poll results during the last several days of the campaign or to prohibit election night projections based on exit polls.

Currently the networks are making projections on the air on election night no sooner than the time at which in-person balloting has stopped in a particular state. This is being done under a "gentlemen's agreement" that does not have the force of law, and Congress has considered ways to formalize this arrangement. In continuing discussions, a feasible proposal to eliminate problems for voters on the West Coast would have uniform poll closings all across the country. This could conceivably be done together with establishment of a uniform number of hours that the polls must be open in each precinct. In this manner, all the votes would be cast before news organizations made a burst of projections. Such a law would be very disruptive to the current administration of elections in the United States, and it would involve a substantial increase in costs for some jurisdictions. Therefore, such a law is not likely to pass in Congress until solutions are found for these problems.

In many foreign countries without our Bill of Rights, however, laws forbid the publication of preelection polls late in the campaign—for the last two weeks in France, for example, or for the weekend before the election in Canada. And other laws prohibit projections based on exit polls. But these restrictions will not be adopted in the United States.

References

BARTELS, LARRY M. 1988. *Presidential Primaries and the Dynamics of Public Choice.* Princeton: Princeton University Press.
This book offers the best description of how the current presidential nomination process works. It focuses on the post-1972 period in which the candidates have been required to enter primaries and caucuses in order to secure pledged delegates at their parties' national nominating conventions. Bartels deals with the concept of *momentum*—its value to candidates and the impact it has on voters.

One of the key concepts explaining voter choice in the primaries is the set of expectations created by the candidates and the press in concert. Voters are looking for cues about whom to support, which can come from various sources, including political elites, the results in previous primaries or caucuses, and polls. The quantification of the opinions of others in polls has become one of the greatest contributors to the media's propensity to engage in "horserace" coverage that describes who is ahead and who is behind. And this makes a substantial contribution to momentum and perceptions of viability.

CANTRIL, ALBERT H. 1991. *The Opinion Connection: Polling, Politics, and the Press.* Washington, D.C.: CQ Press.
This highly readable book was written under the auspices of the National Council on Public Polls (NCPP), a professional organization of survey firms dedicated to improving both the quality of polls and the quality of poll-based information that is publicly disseminated. It was written, in part, in response to the wave of criticism that "the polls" and their usage by the news media received during the 1988 Bush-Dukakis election campaign. Cantril was chosen by NCPP because of his reputation as an expert on survey methods and their relationship to news and politics.

The book is both scholarly and comprehensive. Scholarly, in that it is informed by expert opinion and by research findings on poll methods effects and reports many of these opinions and findings. Comprehensive, in that it provides a historical perspective on the issues it addresses and succeeds in addressing the issues in an interrelated fashion. For example, there is a chapter that tracks the "reciprocal effects" among polls, the media, and politics. Long sections in the book guide the reader toward a better understanding of the strengths and limitations of polling methods and an appreciation of the potential benefits that poll-based information can have in a democracy.

CANTRIL, ALBERT H., ED. 1980. *Polling on the Issues*. Carson, Calif.: Seven Locks Press.
This book is a report from a conference held in November 1979 under the sponsorship of the Kettering Foundation. It presents the proceedings of each of four sessions in the form of fourteen summaries of presentations or sets of comments.

The first session looked at "Polling: Journalism or Social Science?" and included presentations on the impact of journalism on polling and the impact of polling on journalism. The second section includes five presentations on the uses and analysis of polling data, ranging from politics to commercial products. The third section summarizes a round table on the impact of polls on the policy environment. The final section consists of presentations made by George Gallup, Harry O'Neill, and Mervin Field on polling as a political institution, focusing on the use of polls to support representative government and the obligations of pollsters to collect and present data in the public interest.

CRESPI, IRVING. 1988. *Pre-Election Polling: Sources of Accuracy and Error*. New York: Russell Sage Foundation.
This is probably the single best treatment of the impact of methodology on the accuracy of preelection polling. After an extended discussion of the sources of error in these polls, it ultimately employs a multivariate analysis to see which factors are most conducive to the production of accurate estimates of election outcomes.

Crespi conducted both a qualitative and a quantitative analysis of poll results as predictions of election outcomes by organizing a "survey" of pollsters who conduct preelection polls. In all, he evaluates 430 surveys of different elections, looking at the final preelection estimates in relation to the actual division of the vote.

Forty years after the industry encountered problems with the preelection polls leading up to the 1948 election, Crespi concludes that the same four major sources of error are still present: flawed sample designs, inadequate screening of likely voters, inadequate methods for dealing with "undecided" voters, and failure to measure late changes or shifts in the electorate. Two major sources of difficulty are a lack of commitment to high standards by media organizations who sponsor preelection polls and a willingness by pollsters to engage in judgmental interpretation of their data rather than rely narrowly on accurate measurement.

HERBST, SUSAN. 1993. *Numbered Voices: How Public Opinion Has Shaped American Politics.* Chicago: University of Chicago Press.
In this book, Herbst traces the history of quantification in American journalism as it is inextricably linked to coverage of campaigns and elections. She covers straw polls and problems of crowd estimation, as precursors to the movement toward polling as we know it today. In that regard, she sees polls as a sociological phenomenon that are a natural development of other forces that have been at work in our political system. This part of the book is enhanced by the results of interviews with journalists who represent different cohorts of political reporters.

The focus is almost entirely on preelection polls and their role in structuring campaign coverage. While the movement toward polling is clear in the context of today's journalism, there is simultaneously a movement toward the use of more qualitative methods, such as focus groups.

MANN, THOMAS E., AND GARY R. ORREN, EDS. 1992. *Media Polls in American Politics.* Washington D.C.: Brookings Institution.
Mann and Orren, in their introductory chapter, "To Poll or Not to Poll," set the stage for this volume by briefly chronicling American media polling back to the early nineteenth century. They summarize the potential strengths of poll results as news and many actual problems with the way this information is often used. Most of the other chapters offer variations on this theme, but with a reinforcing, rather than redundant, effect.

A theme addressed by at least four of the chapters, directly or indirectly, is that a number from a poll should never be the lead of a news story; instead, the findings of a reliable poll should be treated by journalists as a source, and preferably not the only source, for the story. This includes the chapters by E.J. Dionne (*Washington Post*), Michael Kagay (*New York Times*), and Kathleen Frankovic (CBS News).

The chapter by Michael Traugott is the most comprehensive critical review to date of the considerable literature on the impact of polling news on the public. Traugott observes that "after all the evidence is reviewed, it is difficult to escape the conclusions that [preelection] media polls do affect the public."

Ultimately, a clear message from the book is that polls can and should be a highly valued sources of news, but journalists' poll-based coverage is too often lacking in methodological rigor and analytically inadequate, and is placed in too narrow a context.

MOORE, DAVID W. 1992. *The Superpollsters*. New York: Four Walls Eight Windows.

This is an important book because it personalizes the contemporary polling business through fascinating recountings of several important figures in the business. In addition to chapters about such major public pollsters as George Gallup and Louis Harris, the reader can find information about the major Democratic pollsters—Pat Caddell, Peter Hart, and Irwin "Tubby" Harrison—as well as Republican pollsters Robert Teeter and Richard Wirthlin. On the media side, the major figures portrayed include Warren Mitofsky (CBS and VRS), Richard Morin (*Washington Post*), Michael Kagay (*New York Times*), Kathleen Frankovic (CBS), and Jeff Alderman (ABC).

These chapters provide an interesting perspective on how the commercial side of the polling business has developed through descriptions of the career paths of critical figures involved in it. Most of the chapters present very favorable portrayals, the notable exceptions being the reviews of Louis Harris and Shere Hite.

3

How Do Political Candidates and Organizations Use Poll Data?

The main difference between polls conducted for candidates and media polls is that the former are conducted for private, strategic use, while the latter are used for news analysis. Sometimes the results of private polls are leaked to the press because they serve a candidate's interests—either in support of his or her own candidacy, as a way of influencing coverage or perceptions of an opponent, or as way to influence campaign contributions. Because of their strategic use in the campaign, the results of candidate polls are usually kept confidential.

One problem with making the results of campaign polls public is that they often involve questions designed to evaluate strategic alternatives—"what if" kinds of questions. The campaign may never carry out some (or even most) of these possible strategies, in part because of what the poll results show. Therefore, the responses to these questions are not meaningful or valid for inferring public reactions to the candidates, and they are kept private so the campaign does not divulge its strategic intent.

Another problem with campaign polls is that they are often conducted with samples of voters that are unrepresentative of the general population. That is, a campaign may be interested in the attitudes or expected voting behavior of "independent" or "undecided" voters, or people who voted for the candidate the last time he or she ran. These results cannot obviously be generalized to the entire electorate. Sometimes such inferences are made, however, because of deception in the campaign or because reporters are not savvy enough to be able to distinguish the appropriate reference population.

How often do candidates use polls?

Research is an important part of every political campaign, and candidates like to have as much information as possible at a reasonable cost. Since polling costs money, the number of polls conducted during a particular campaign depends on the available resources.

In presidential contests, each candidate will have tens of polls conducted across the eighteen to twenty-four months of serious campaigning. In the prenomination phase, the campaign needs to obtain information on the relative standing and "image" of its candidate, alone and in relation to the others. This information may also be useful in stimulating contributions to the campaign and dissuading contributors to the opponent's campaign.[5] In a presidential campaign, this information has only limited value at the national level because the real contest takes place on a state-by-state basis through the primaries and caucuses. The primary process is "front loaded" so the events in such early states as New Hampshire and Iowa are unusually important. Therefore, most candidates seeking the nomination will have polling data from these states. They will continue to collect data like this as long as they remain in the fight for the nomination.

At the point that one of the candidates seems to have the nomination in hand, usually in the early spring, the emphasis may turn temporarily to national polls. These will include assessments of how the candidate will fare against the likely nominee of the other party. In other words, the emphasis will shift temporarily

5. Diana E. Mutz, "Media, Momentum, and Money: Horse Race Spin in the 1988 Republican Primaries," in *Presidential Polls and the News Media*, ed. Paul J. Lavrakas, Michael W. Traugott, and Peter V. Miller (Boulder, Colo.: Westview Press, 1995), 229–54.

from local to national standing. By the time the general election campaign is well under way, however, just after the nominating conventions, the emphasis will shift back to state-level polls, as success on Election Day depends on winning a majority of the electoral votes (winning enough states to total 270 electoral votes). During the general election campaign, there will be a lot of national polling available through media organizations at no cost to the candidates.

As Election Day approaches, candidate polls increasingly emphasize the results of the trial-heat question as the campaign strives to do whatever is necessary to carry a state. Because a presidential campaign is conducted on a fixed budget determined by federal law, the campaign is continuously faced with resource allocation issues: Should we invest our next $100,000 in television or direct mail? Are we better off to increase our advertising budget in New York or California? Should we cut back on our expenditures in Florida and increase our effort in Arizona? Information obtained through polls helps answer these kinds of questions.

Allowing for differences in the procedures by which candidates seek nomination and organize their general election campaigns, all of these same processes play themselves out at the state level for local candidates.

How do candidates use polls?

Candidates use polls for many purposes. First, campaigns use polls to learn what the important issues are in the minds of the voters. Such poll results provide a broad picture of the thematic content of the campaign (What issues do I have to discuss?), they are also a way to highlight the relative strengths of the candidate and the opposition in terms of the positions they have taken on these issues (What issues are the strongest for me? Which ones advantage my opponent?)

Candidates also use polls to evaluate the ways in which elements of the thematic content of their campaigns are resonating with members of the electorate. Most successful candidates have held elective office, so their policy positions on many issues are well known because they have developed over time. These are typically reflected in a series of votes the candidate cast or speeches he or she made that indicate where he or she stands. So candidates do not usually employ polls to decide what positions they should take. This does not mean, however, that candidates do not use polls to evaluate the popularity of different or alternative positions they might take on an issue, or to evaluate the impact of different ways of discussing the issues. They may use this information to alter their emphasis or the language they use to discuss issues of particular importance to them or the electorate.

Developing a "positive image" means that a candidate is well known and well liked. Therefore the campaign also needs continuous monitoring of how well recognized the candidate is, whether or not the electorate looks on him or her favorably, and the relative standing of the candidates from opposing parties. By collecting these data over time, the campaign management team can gauge the effectiveness of their efforts and decide whether strategy should be changed or more effort put into advertising, for example.

Are polls the only technique for collecting information during a campaign?

Polls are an effective way to collect certain kinds of information, but there are other important ways to do campaign research. Some of these include analyzing historical voting patterns in precincts and cities across the constituency, reviewing successful advertising strategies from past campaigns, and keeping track of news coverage of the campaign.

Focus groups are commonly used by campaigns to get a sense of how things are going. Eight to ten people are assembled for a group discussion organized around a particular topic. A set of campaign themes might be evaluated for presentation in political ads, for example. Focus groups can provide very important information to a campaign that is richer in detail than the information obtained in polls.

In a poll, a representative sample of people is drawn from a larger population to which inferences can be drawn. So a scientific sample of likely voters might be drawn to learn what they are thinking or are likely to do. Each person is asked exactly the same questions to facilitate comparison of responses. If a good sample has been used, the results from the poll—such as the percentage of people who know who the candidate is—can be inferred to the population as a whole.

In a focus group, people are assembled for a broad-ranging discussion about a limited set of topics, but they are encouraged to do this in their own language in response to broad, open-end questions. Campaigns use focus groups to develop an understanding of what kinds of things people are thinking about, but not to estimate how many people hold each kind of view. This is why focus groups are used to evaluate the effectiveness of ads—whether the intended message is being conveyed in the desired way.

Do the results of campaign polls depend on when they are conducted?

The results of polls do depend on when they are conducted, in a variety of ways. First, polls conducted early in the campaign, during the primaries and before, will produce results favorable to the best-known candidates. Recognition is a minimum condition for evaluation, which in turn must precede support. So early in the campaign, the best-known candidates will generally have higher favorability ratings, and they will do better in the trial-heat questions that evaluate the candidates' relative standing. Later in the campaign, poll results reflect a more reliable assessment of how the candidates are doing, when all who remain are relatively well known.

Skillful candidates and their managers can take advantage of such poll results to promote their own candidacies and to try to hurt their opponents. One critical way campaigns do this is to try to stimulate more financial contributions when the polls suggest they are doing well and to dissuade contributors from giving to another candidate when the polls show their opponent doing poorly.

In presidential politics this is a highly effective strategy in the pre-nomination phase when the candidates have to raise most of their money on their own. In the general election campaign, the candidates receive federal funds (about $63 million each in 1996) and cannot raise money for themselves, so this effect is not present.

Do the results of campaign polls depend on how they are conducted?

The results of campaign polls, just like any other kind of poll, are highly sensitive to the way in which they are conducted. That means the results of polls can be manipulated by altering the data-collection methodology.

Because of the relationship between candidate recognition and support, for example, the wording of questions can make a lot of difference in the level of support that a candidate receives. Early in the campaign, an open-end question in the form of "Who would you like to see win the Republican (or Democratic) nomination for president?" will result in quite different (and lower) support levels for a relatively unknown candidate than a question worded this way:

> Here is a list of candidates seeking the Republican (Democratic) nomination for president. Which of these would you like to see win the nomination?

Lesser-known candidates often use results from the second form of this question to launch their campaigns, by showing voters (and reporters and potential contributors) that they have reasonable levels of support in the electorate. Again, this could represent a case where untrained journalists report opinions suggesting a level of candidate support that is an artifact of question wording. If the question were asked a different way, the results would be different.

Do candidates use poll results in strategic ways?

The main purpose of campaign polls is to provide information on what the campaign should do or how effective its actions have been, so campaign polls are always used strategically. The results from campaign polls can be used to evaluate the strengths of one side and the weaknesses of the other; how well an ad campaign is working; or whether a response is needed to an issue raised in the media or by an opponent.

The *release* of poll results can also be used strategically to foster a candidacy or to harm an opponent. Press conference or leaks of results might suggest that one candidate is gaining ground or doing better or that an opponent is losing ground or doing worse —in general or especially among an important electoral group such as women or independents or people who are most likely to vote.

Can candidate polls be misleading?

Because campaign polls often evaluate strategic alternatives, the release of results, especially in small snippets of information, can be misleading. Candidates sometimes collect data through a form of "push poll" in which they ask a series of hypothetical questions about their opponents. For example, they might ask questions concerning little-known facts about an opponent's personal life or positions on particular issues.

These questions are often asked in a series that takes the following general form:

> *a.* If the election were held today, which candidate would you prefer?
> *b.* Suppose you learned (a statement) about candidate A. Would you still support him?
> *c.* Suppose you learned (another statement) about candidate A. Would you still support him?
> [After a series of such questions]
> *d.* If the election were held today, which candidate would you prefer?

In this sequence, these successive revelations are used to evaluate what kinds of things a campaign might emphasize or disclose in order to move or "push" support away from an opponent. But the campaign may never actually try such a strategy, some of the "revelations" may not be exactly true, or the opponent may have a reasonable explanation for the potential charge. So the results of this kind of poll should not be straightforwardly extrapolated to the public campaign. These issues are discussed in greater detail in chapter 10.

Can media poll results help a candidate?

In an election campaign, there is no substitute for good news. Poll results that show a candidate ahead or gaining momentum can stimulate contributions or volunteers, energize the staff, or even stimulate voter turnout at the end of the campaign. The candidates and their staffs will try to get the media to repeat these results as often as possible in order to generate a more positive "spin" that will help their image. So good poll results have clear benefits for a campaign.

Can media poll results hurt a candidate?

A good deal of reporting on public affairs involves the use of sporting metaphors: Who is ahead or behind? Who is gaining or falling back? What are the odds that a candidate can win it all on Election Day? Together with this, there is a tendency for people to want to back a winner or to try harder when they think their side has a chance to win, as opposed to being hopelessly behind.

Election coverage is filled with messages like this. Many of them come from the campaigns themselves, including the candidates, their managers, and party officials. A good deal come from political columnists and pundits. Some of them come from polls. When election polls show that one candidate is trailing badly, and the commentary suggests that the outlook is bleak, the campaign can be hurt by poll results. They can have the effect of slowing or completely drying up the flow of funds or reducing the number of volunteers.

In these instances, the campaign staff will try to produce an explanation or "spin" that minimizes the damage that such polls can produce.

How do political parties use polls?

Political parties sometimes conduct their own polls to check their standing with the electorate and to augment the information available to their candidates. A state party may conduct a poll on how the governor's race and the contests for the state legislature are going, and they may also ask about the presidential race. If they supply this information to a presidential campaign, it may have to be counted as a contribution "in kind" to the candidate.

Late in the campaign, the party is interested in finding out who is likely to vote and which candidates they are likely to support. Polls are used in such efforts as an important part of "get out the vote" (GOTV) drives. Without ever asking about the presidential contest (because it might be seen as an in-kind contribution under federal campaign laws), the party can ask questions that enable them to classify respondents as "likely Democratic" or "likely Republican" voters. They use this information to contact the most likely voters on Election Day to see whether or not they have gone to vote yet; often they will offer their likely voters a ride to their balloting places. By delivering a likely partisan to the local balloting location, they have a good idea of how that person will vote for president too.

Why do special-interest groups use polls?

By the very nature of their organization, special-interest groups have a desire to influence legislation, regulation, or public policy concerning matters of interest to their members. Therefore, special-interest groups use polls for a variety of purposes: to maintain contact with their members and to find out where they stand on a particular issue; to collect information from the public to see where it stands on a particular issue; or to collect and distribute information to public policymakers.

These are all legitimate goals for such an organization to pursue. When a special-interest group collects data for internal management and research purposes, this is no different from a corporation's collecting marketing data for its products. If the data are made public, however, it is appropriate to apply a series of evaluative criteria for the purpose of deciding how much weight to give such information. This is especially important when the leaders of the group suggest that the poll results reflect broad public opinion on an issue. For example, it is usually inappropriate to characterize the opinions of the members of the group, who have joined because of their common interests, as a reflection of "public opinion" or "what Americans think" on a topic.

Some special-interest groups also include *pseudo polls* with highly biased questions in their mass mailings. Under the guise of survey research, some organizations send out letters that look like they contain surveys, for the purpose of soliciting new members (known as "Soliciting Under the Guise" of survey research, or SUGing) or raising money (known as "Fund Raising Under the Guise" of survey research, or FRUGing). These are inappropriate uses of the survey method, according to the American Association for Public Opinion Research (AAPOR) and the National Council of Public Polls (NCPP). These organizations frequently make public comments about especially egregious examples of such misuse. Issues of interpretation and evaluation are discussed in greater detail in chapter 10.

Are there problems with some polls conducted by special-interest groups?

There could be a problem because any advocacy group is typically interested in advancing an agenda. This means these groups could be inclined to use nonprobability or otherwise unrepresentative samples and/or biased question wordings to collect data that support their position on an issue.

For these reasons, it is useful if not imperative that a consumer of polls always know who sponsored a poll and what questions were asked of whom. Any responsible group should be willing to identify itself as a sponsor of research and to provide full methodological information on how any polls that it sponsored were conducted. This would include a description of the sample design (who the respondents were and how they were chosen) and a copy of the complete questionnaire that gives full question wordings and the order in which they were presented (what the respondents were asked).

References

MARTIN, L. JOHN, ED. 1984. "Polling and the Democratic Consensus." *Annals of the American Academy of Political and Social Science* 472 (March). This volume is an early compendium of articles on the role of polls in the democratic process. The work is divided into four parts, consisting of thirteen articles.

The first section is devoted to public opinion polling as a technique and the kinds of measures it produces. These articles include discussions of how polls are conducted, their accuracy, trends in public opinion in the United States, and the relationships between public opinion, polling, and political behavior.

The second section includes articles on polls and politicians, emphasizing presidential politics but including an article about congressional and state and local elections. The section on polls and the media includes two articles, focusing on polling as a news-gathering tool and the impact of polling on mass media organizations. The last section covers the impact of polls on the public and includes one of the few extant articles on polls and ethnic minorities.

SABATO, LARRY J. 1981. *The Rise of Political Consultants.* New York: Basic Books. This is one of the few books that contains a collection of information about the new breed of professionals who work in contemporary political campaigns and the range of services they provide. Chapter 2 is devoted to "The Pols and Polls," and it contains a discussion of the history of political polling, descriptions of the kinds and costs of polls conducted for candidates, the use of polls in campaigns, and the use of polls in governing.

4

How Do News Organizations Collect and Report Poll Data?

Media organizations collectively spend millions of dollars for polls during election campaigns so that they can produce content for news stories. Some news organizations purchase data from market research firms by underwriting the costs of a special survey, while others subscribe to a nationally syndicated service such as the Gallup or Harris polls. The largest news organizations in the country —the television networks and major metropolitan daily newspapers like the *New York Times* and the *Washington Post*—have their own polling units. And many of them operate in partnership with each other when they do not compete directly for the same audience.

Election coverage has always been a "good story" for news organizations. Elections have high impact on their audience members. They occur on a schedule that facilitates planning the coverage and assigning resources to it. Campaigns involve conflict, and they are filled with willing sources who will talk to reporters. And campaigns are always resolved on Election Day, when winners and losers are declared. Election polls contribute to many of these characteristics of campaign coverage as it has existed for much longer than polls have been around. But journalists are happy to use poll data in their stories because they support many of the tendencies and reporting styles they like to use.

Why do media organizations conduct polls?

There are three main reasons that media organizations conduct their own polls. First, they like to have editorial control over the content and timing of the surveys, exercising their own judgment over news decisions and values. Second, they enjoy the professional prestige that comes from their peers' acknowledgment of the quality of their polls. This occurs when other news organizations pick up their stories or cite their poll results in stories they produce. Third, they use poll results to inform and structure their subsequent reporting of the campaign.

Recent research shows that all major newspapers use polls in reporting, and the vast majority sponsor their own polls. Among those who do not sponsor polls, the most frequently cited explanation is that financial resources are not available; otherwise they would. Television stations are increasingly making use of local polls as well.

In the "old days" that extended from the 1940s to the 1970s, many news organizations subscribed to syndicated services that provided regular signed columns produced by national polling figures such as George Gallup or Louis Harris. The newspapers received one or two prepackaged news stories each week, based on data collected by these organizations, usually through face-to-face interviews. With the arrival of low-cost telephone surveys, news organizations realized that they could conduct their own polls at reasonable cost, whenever they wanted and covering whatever topics they wanted. This meant they could exercise independent news judgments about when current events suggested they should field a poll and what questions they should ask.

How do polls contribute to good journalism?

Elections are a fundamental part of American democracy because they involve the selection and replacement of our representatives. Most people are not interested in politics most of the time, but the activity of a campaign stimulates periodic bursts of interest, leading right up to Election Day when voters go to the polls. Campaigns and elections are an important part of news coverage because of their relevance to American political life. They also occur on a well-known schedule according to a well-understood set of regulations. All of this makes them easy and important to cover. There is conflict between the opposing candidates but then a clear resolution on Election Day. This also makes it easy for news media to organize their coverage.

Polls contribute to journalism by providing an independent perspective on citizens' views about the candidates and issues involved in election campaigns. Every campaign has willing sources who will discuss their strategy and prospects. But we have come to understand that these political elites (candidates, campaign managers, party chairs, and the like) put their own "spin" on these assessments. They try to make their own chances look as good as possible and their opponents' as poor as possible.

Well-conducted surveys provide another perspective on the dynamics of the campaign and popular assessments of the candidates, as well as an independent view of the effectiveness of their efforts. A random sample of voters, representative of the electorate at large, can provide an untainted view of what is going on and what is likely to happen on Election Day. Election polls also provide a perspective on what issues are important to the voters, and how these interests relate to what the candidates are discussing.

Why do media organizations collaborate on polling?

The main reason that media organizations collaborate on polls is to share the costs. These partnerships began twenty years ago when the *New York Times* and CBS News joined to conduct polls together for the 1976 election. The newspaper had an important resource in the telephone banks in its advertising department that were unused at night, when most of the interviewing was done. This first arrangement was followed by one between ABC News and the *Washington Post*. A third, between NBC News and the *Wall Street Journal,* now involves data collected by outsiders.

Furthermore, these early partnerships involved major metropolitan dailies with morning circulation and networks with evening news broadcasts. Both shared a common deadline of late afternoon/early evening, though their products appeared on two separate days. This meant that each organization could have access to the data simultaneously. The networks presented the results first but in abbreviated form because a television story is generally shorter than a newspaper story on the same topic. The newspapers presented the story a few hours later but in greater detail.

In the first partnership, the television story was described as the product of a CBS News/*New York Times* poll. The next morning's story was described as the product of a *New York Times*/CBS poll.

Currently, there are partnerships between local newspapers and television stations, and some between weekly news magazines and networks. In the latter case, the stories typically appear on a Sunday evening on television and in the magazine on Monday when it hits the newsstand.

Are there special pressures that affect media polls?

Yes there are, because the news is a "product" that is generally produced on a twenty-four-hour cycle, which is getting even shorter through advanced technology, the continuous production of network television news on CNN, and local "around-the-clock" news stations. So in order for poll results to be "news," they have to be fresh and reflect content that was not made obsolete by events in the real world since the data were collected.

As a result, media polls have to be collected in a relatively short field period. Typically this means data collected in forty-eight to seventy-two hours, across two or three nights of interviewing. One consequence is that response rates in media polls are typically lower than in surveys conducted across longer field periods. There is less time available to recontact potential respondents who were not home or refused to be interviewed the first time they were contacted. A reduced response rate is a clear tradeoff that news organizations accept in order to collect and report timely information. These issues are discussed in greater detail in chapter 5.

What are the standard data-collection methods used in media polling?

The typical media poll is based on telephone interviews, usually collected during the evening hours across a few days. The samples of phone numbers are purchased. They consist either of a combination of telephone numbers taken from listings in directories plus other, randomly selected numbers or entirely of numbers randomly selected by computer. The major news organizations employ various techniques for selecting a particular respondent within a household where they make contact. Less reliable methods involve conducting an interview with whoever answers the phone.

Media polls usually employ relatively brief interviews, sometimes lasting as little as ten minutes and rarely extending for more than half an hour. Most of the questions are "closed-end": the respondent is asked to select an answer from a limited number that are offered. Rarely do these surveys employ "open-end" questions in which the respondent answers in his or her own words, because they take longer to administer and require additional coding that can slow down the analysis of the data. Details of questionnaires are discussed in chapter 7.

Computer assisted telephone interviewing (CATI) systems are currently the preferred means of conducting telephone polls. The interviewer reads the questions from a computer monitor and records the answer directly into the computer database. When the interview is completed, the data record for that respondent is immediately ready for analysis. When the last interview is conducted, there is an entire data set, consisting of the responses from every person interviewed, ready for analysis.

Some news organizations collect data by methodologies that they inappropriately call "polls." These include "call-in" polls where readers or viewers are encouraged to call in to "800" numbers (free to the caller) or even "900" numbers (that cost the caller) or "mail-in" polls where readers are asked to complete questionnaires inserted in magazines or newspapers. These techniques and their problems are discussed in greater detail in chapter 10.

Results from these kinds of polls should be ignored. These

techniques almost always produce biased and completely unrepresentative data because they do not involve scientific samples.

Can the methodology of media polls have an impact on the results?

The methodology of media polls does not have to have an impact on the results, although sometimes it may. It is very difficult to assess in quantitative terms what the impact might be, compared to other methods.

On some topics, a short field period that results in a low response rate can produce biased results because people who are readily available and willing to give an interview may differ from people who are unavailable during that short time period. Some news organizations try to collect data in one night, or even across a few hours between the early evening news and the eleven o'clock edition. This can be extremely problematical and is likely to introduce substantial bias in the data.

Surveys based entirely on closed-end questions that do not allow respondents to answer in their own language and with their own frame of reference can sometimes produce biased results. This is especially true if the response categories do not appropriately reflect the types of opinions held by the public.

How are media polls analyzed and disseminated?

Media polls are analyzed with the use of statistical software written for computers. Usually the analysis is not very complicated because it is difficult to produce timely news stories based on complex analysis, but sometimes more extensive reports are prepared and disseminated.

Analysis begins by looking at the "marginals" or frequency distribution for each question in the survey. This provides such information as how many men and women are in the sample or how many approve or disapprove of Bill Clinton's handling of his job as president.

The next step is to run cross tabulations by looking at the joint distribution of the responses to two questions (the bivariate frequencies), the most rudimentary form of analysis. This provides such information as how many (what proportion of) men approve of Bill Clinton's handling of his job as president, compared to how many women do so. In rare instances, a third question, such as party identification, is added to the analysis. This technique addresses such questions as whether Republican women approve of Bill Clinton at the same level as Democratic women.

The vast majority of analysis of media polls consists of the presentation of marginals for the entire sample. A small proportion consists of bivariate analysis, and almost no analysis is presented in terms of the effects of third variables. Sometimes data are presented in tabular form, but most often, the results are presented as descriptive statements in the printed or spoken text.

Do reports of poll results differ when presented on television or in newspapers?

The typical poll-based story on television consists of a voice-over in which an anchor or commentator is talking about the results as data are presented on the screen. Sometimes the commentator is speaking as file footage is presented to illustrate the main point of the analysis, such as pictures of voters going to vote or of the candidates.

Newspaper stories based on polls are longer and involve more detailed analysis. Because they have more space to present results, newspapers often recontact survey respondents and have them amplify on the views they expressed in the survey. Sometimes, these stories will also include pictures of the respondents at home or at work, in an attempt to personalize the findings beyond the aggregated statistics derived from the poll.

Can media polls conducted by different news organizations produce different results?

Yes, they can and often do. The simplest explanation for these differences is that the two polls used different samples or questions or that they were conducted at different times. During the campaign, some polls are based on interviews with samples of adults eighteen and over, while others are based on interviews only with adults registered to vote. Since only about two out of three adults are registered, these different populations can produce different results, even when all other things are equal.

Even if the samples are similar, the questions may be different enough to produce seemingly different results. One survey may ask about approval of how Bill Clinton is handling his job as president; another may ask about approval of his handling of the economy. Newspaper stories prepared from these polls could have quite different headlines referring to "Clinton approval ratings."

The order in which the questions are asked can also have an effect on the results. The Gallup Organization, which "invented" the presidential approval question, always asks this question first in its surveys so no other question can affect the results. Research has shown that asking questions about the economy, for example, produces different responses to the presidential approval question than not, depending on whether the nation's economy is in good condition or poor shape.

Obviously public opinion can change over time because of intervening events. So two news organizations could report polls conducted a few weeks apart in a period when a major international event took place. Whether this event reflected positively or negatively on the president could explain differences in his approval ratings, all other things being equal. During the prenomination campaign, when primaries are occurring almost every week, how well a candidate did in last week's primaries can affect his evaluations this week.

Issues of question wording and question order are discussed in greater detail in chapter 7.

Why are there so many polls reported in the media?

Because polls provide such interesting and useful information for journalists, news organizations are inclined to use their results when they are available. The news is often about conflict and is filled with sports metaphors about who is ahead or behind and why. The reporting of poll results, especially for the trial-heat question about who is ahead, naturally lends itself to this emphasis on horserace journalism.

Many news organizations produce their own survey data, and often these results enter the general news stream through the wire services or syndicated columns. But there are other sources of polling data during a campaign. The candidates are always conducting surveys, and they frequently provide results to reporters, sometimes through carefully orchestrated leaks. Of course they are more likely to do this when they think they have information to bolster their candidacy.

American politics is increasingly characterized by the activity of organized special-interest groups, and these groups often sponsor polls on topics of particular interest to them. These groups then prepare press releases or hold press conferences to present their poll results. Since a good deal of the news comes from coverage of such events, this is another avenue for polls to get into the news.

Finally, there is some research suggesting that the focus of campaign coverage has changed, with a growing emphasis on the strategy and dynamics of the campaign.[6] Many candidates and their managers attribute their own or their opponent's behavior to movements in reaction to poll results. At the same time, reporters describe actions candidates take or visits they make as necessary because "the polls" show they needed to strengthen their position among a particular group of voters.

Research shows that these generic references to polls, without any citation of source or actual data, are a growing element in campaign coverage. This can be a special problem for voters interested in substantive issues in the campaign who can only find coverage of the dynamics and strategy of the campaign. Some critics argue that a preponderance of news preoccupied with candidates behaving in a strategic fashion with regard to each other and not responding to

6. Thomas Patterson, *Out of Order* (New York: Knopf, 1993).

the voters' interests in issues has led to a growing cynicism about government and declining turnout.

References

GAWISER, SHELDON R., AND G. EVANS WITT. 1994. *A Journalist's Guide to Public Opinion Polls.* Westport, Conn.: Praeger.
This book is intended as a brief introduction to polling for journalists who are responsible for writing about polls—from their own news organizations or sponsored by candidates or interest groups. It is written in a style that is accessible to any educated reader.

There are eighteen chapters in the book. The first five cover the history of polling in journalism, focusing on the new trend toward precision journalism. The next seven chapters provide information on how to evaluate a particular poll, based on who sponsored it or collected the data, with what kind of sample, and looking at the major sources of error that could arise. There is a specific chapter devoted to pseudo polls and SLOP. There are also four chapters that provide advice on how to report on a poll, including one devoted to exit polls and election night projections. One of the appendixes is especially helpful because it contains a list of twenty questions that need to be answered in order to make an independent evaluation of a poll.

GOLLIN, ALBERT E., GUEST ED. 1980. "Polls and the News Media: A Symposium," *Public Opinion Quarterly* 44, no. 4 (Winter 1980).
This special issue of *Public Opinion Quarterly* consists of eleven articles devoted entirely to the use of polls by the news media. In his introduction, Gollin discusses the increase in media-conducted polls and their potential for altering standard patterns of political coverage. Articles by Crespi and by Weaver and McCombs explore the relationship between pollsters and the press, the use of polls in the press, and how this has changed over time.

In the next section, four articles examine the uses and effects of polls based on content analysis of polls in the media. Articles by Paletz et al. and Broh compare the presentation of polls in the *New York Times* and on network news. Lang and Lang look at polls on a particular topic—Watergate—and the contest for public opinion that was waged in the press, including the use of polls. Worcester contributes a comparative analysis of the use of polling techniques and the presentation of poll results in England in the context of parliamentary elections. Kovach concludes the section with a discussion of the use of polls from an editor's perspective.

In the final section, three articles present critiques and appraisals of the role of polls in the media. Von Hoffman's concern is that newspapers are using polls to make news. Ladd discusses the conflict between the institutional imperatives of the media and pollsters that often produces conflicts between them. In the final article, Noelle-Neumann again provides a comparative perspective on the movement toward "precision journalism."

LAVRAKAS, PAUL J., AND JACK K. HOLLEY, EDS. 1991. *Polling and Presidential Election Coverage.* Newbury Park, Calif.: Sage.
This edited book focuses on the use of poll-based coverage in the 1988 Bush-Dukakis election campaign. It contains an introductory chapter, summarizing the contents, and nine original chapters, most of which were written by either top media-based pollsters or major political consultants.

Three themes unite the chapters: (1) How did the news media use pre-election polls to cover the Bush-Dukakis election? (2) What effects did this coverage likely have on the public? (3) What might the media and journalists do better in using polls as part of their future election coverage?

The book contains the first publications of their kind on how the *New York Times* uses polls to organize its election campaign coverage (by Michael Kagay); how the major exit polls were conducted (by Warren Mitofsky); and a critical review of the "performance" of journalists and their pollsters (by the late I.A. "Bud" Lewis). For those interested in a theoretical modeling of the plausible effects of election polls, there is a chapter by political strategist Harrison Hickman. Finally, two other chapters provide the first national perspective on what the American public thinks about elections polls and their use by the news media.

LAVRAKAS, PAUL J., MICHAEL W. TRAUGOTT, AND PETER V. MILLER, EDS. 1995. *Presidential Polls and the News Media.* Boulder, Colo.: Westview Press.
This book focuses almost entirely on the 1992 Bush-Clinton-Perot election campaign. There is an introduction that summarizes each chapter and links them together along the lines of (1) developments in media polling; (2) the methods of media polls; (3) media polls in the 1992 elections; and (4) the public's reaction to media polls.

The final chapter identifies four common themes in the book: the "power of the polls"; the notion that the media are mostly "data rich but analysis poor"; the need for a "new approach" to using polls and related research techniques, in the form of focus groups, to both frame and make news; and the need for the news media to exercise greater responsibility in using and reporting election poll-based news so as to further, not hinder, democratic processes.

The original contributions include chapters on the effects of pre-primary polls, campaign finances, and candidate viability (by political scientist Diana Mutz); a critique of the media's use of polls in their 1992 election coverage, including the efforts of the author's own paper (by *Washington Post* pollster Richard Morin); an explanation of how focus groups were used by the *Detroit News* to supplement its polling and other election coverage (by Michael Traugott); a self-critique of the national exit polls conducted by Voter Research & Surveys for the networks (by exit pollsters Warren Mitofsky and Murray Edelman); and an explanation and critical review of how the media deal with undecides in preelection polls (by Rob Daves of the *Minneapolis Star Tribune* and Sharon Warden of the *Washington Post*.)

MEYER, PHILIP. 1995. *The New Precision Journalism: A Reporter's Introduction to Social Science Methods.* Bloomington: Indiana University Press.
This book is actually the third edition of the classic "precision journalism" text that Meyer first published in 1973. That book, and its later editions, have succeeded in helping to bring social science methods such as survey research into the newsrooms of the world, with more and more journalists using them to supplement traditional news-gathering methods. Meyer is a very good writer and uses many real-world examples of news stories based on social science methods. Thus the book is an interesting read, even for those who fully understand the topics about which the book provides instruction.

The book explains to journalists the "scientific" roots of news gathering and news analysis, trying to convince the many skeptics in the news business that these are techniques they can and should be using.

The book contains an excellent introductory explanation of data analysis and statistics, with more attention devoted to the role of computers in this new edition. The research methods that are explained, through interesting examples, include surveys and election polls, field experiments, and the use of existing databases for secondary analysis. This is a "must read" for any journalist who hopes to use social science techniques in news gathering and wants to produce accurate reports of the findings that can come from analyzing such data.

WILHOIT, G. CLEVELAND, AND DAVID H. WEAVER. 1980. *Newsroom Guide to Polls and Surveys*. Washington, D.C.: American Newspaper Publishers Association.

This is an early introductory guide for journalists about how to interpret and evaluate polls. It is not a guide to conducting polls; instead, it is aimed at helping reporters who come into frequent contact with polling data.

The book is organized in six sections. The first deals with questionnaires and problems of question bias. When reporting on results produced by others, this is one of the central problems that journalists face. In the second section, the authors treat matters of interviewing procedures, followed by sampling procedures. The next two sections deal with evaluating survey results and writing about them, including examples of good and bad reporting of poll results. The book concludes with a list of sixteen specific questions that reporters should have clear answers to before beginning to write about a specific poll.

5

WHY DO POLLSTERS
USE SAMPLES?

One of the most important decisions that every pollster has to make is how to allocate the money available for a survey. There are two critical components to a survey: the number of people to interview and the number of questions to ask. On the one hand, for any given budget, the longer the interview (the more questions asked), the fewer the number of respondents (the people who can be interviewed). On the other hand, the larger the sample size, the less information that can be obtained from each one.

This is a critical decision for pollsters to make because a large sample size provides more precise estimates of how many people prefer one candidate over the other or support or oppose a particular policy, for example, gun control. But being able to ask more questions can provide important explanatory information about *why* the respondents prefer Bill Clinton over Bob Dole or which kinds of people are likely to favor a ban on assault weapons.

Sampling is one of the most important tools that pollsters have at their disposal. A well-drawn, scientific sample allows a pollster to conduct interviews with only a small fraction of a population but to draw inferences from their responses back to the attitudes or behavior of the entire population. But this can be done reliably and with confidence only if the sample is drawn according to certain laws of probability. When these procedures are followed, pollsters can accurately estimate the opinions of the almost 190 million American adults who are citizens or the candidate preferences of

the 110 million Americans who are expected to vote in 1996 with a
sample of only a few thousand respondents.

Many of the concepts underlying sampling are straightforward
and easily understood. But some sampling concepts are almost
counterintuitive, and many people find them confusing. One of the
most important—and confusing—concepts is the fact that the
same-size sample is necessary to produce an accurate estimate of
opinions in a city, a state, or the entire United States. That is, the
precision of an estimate derived from a sample is a function of the
size of the sample—*almost entirely independent of the size of the population it is drawn from.* This concept and other basic principles of
sampling are discussed in the answers to the following questions.

What is sampling?

Sampling is a technique for selecting a subset of units from a population in order to produce an estimate of some attribute or characteristic of the population at a reasonable cost. In polls, the typical
units are individuals, usually adult citizens of the United States. By
using scientific sampling procedures, a representative subset of citizens can be selected for interviewing. The information collected
from people in a sample—such as their preferences for president of
the United States—can be used to estimate the division of the vote
in the entire population on Election Day.

The practice of sampling actually involves two steps. The first
is the design of a scientific sample, and the second is the implementation of the sample in a valid and reliable way. In the first step,
the statistical procedures of probability theory are used to decide
how units will be selected. In the second step, administrative procedures are used to *ensure good selection* so that the sample has a high
response rate, and good coverage is achieved.

What is involved in a sample design?

Three steps are involved in designing a sample. The first is to define the *target population,* the groups of people for which the estimate will be made. The second is to select an appropriate *sampling frame* that contains all the members of the population. It is important to have a clear definition of the target population because it guides the search for an appropriate sampling frame. The third step is to select an appropriate *probability method* of selecting the units from the sampling frame.

The *target population* is the one to which the researchers want to draw inferences. This could be "people who are likely to vote on Election Day." The *sampling frame* contains a list of all of the units, or *elements* as they are sometimes called, in the population, in this case all of the eligible voters. A *probability method of selection* is one in which every element in the frame has a known, nonzero chance of selection. Sometimes all the units have the same chance of selection; other times, they have unequal (but nonzero) chances of selection.

What is the target population for an election poll?

In 1996 preelection surveys, pollsters typically will be interested in measuring the opinions and voting intentions of those Americans who actually will vote in an upcoming primary or in the November general election. This group of Americans represents the target population for the 1996 election polls.

This definition will differ slightly by the phase of the campaign, however. In the beginning, most pollsters will be interested in interviewing U.S. citizens who are eighteen years of age or older. They will not be too concerned about registration status because many of these people still have time to register before the primaries or the general election.

During the summer and into the general election campaign, starting around Labor Day, the population of interest becomes *registered voters*. And as Election Day nears, the target population becomes *likely voters*, or those who have the highest probability of going to the balloting places to vote.

Some data from the 1992 presidential election illustrate how these target populations differ. In 1992, an estimated 55.2 percent of

Americans age eighteen and over voted in the general election in November. This represented an increase of nearly 10 percent over the proportion that voted in the 1988 presidential election (50.2 percent). Nevertheless, this same number of voters represented almost 90 percent of those registered to vote in 1992. That is, most people who are registered actually vote in presidential elections. The real problem for pollsters is to identify those who are registered.

The issue of defining the target population is much more straightforward for the researchers who conduct exit polls for the 1996 primaries and general election. For exit polls, the target population is all people who "turn out" to vote at voting places on Election Day. Since these people are interviewed leaving their balloting places, this definitional problem is reduced substantially.

Technically speaking, the effective population of interest for most 1996 polls will be somewhat narrower in scope. For example, most national polls are limited to residents of the continental United States, and residents of Alaska and Hawaii are excluded from the target population. A major reason for excluding Alaskans and Hawaiians is that the proportion of the U.S. population residing in those two states is very small (less than 1 percent of the total population), and their exclusion has little effect on the estimates of opinions and voting intentions that the 1996 polls will measure. Furthermore, most national election polls conduct telephone interviews from the Eastern and Central time zones, and standard interviewing shifts do not correspond very well with the time zones in Alaska and Hawaii when citizens are likely to be at home. Thus, pollsters make a conscious cost-benefit calculation to trade a little bit of inaccuracy caused by omitting Alaskans and Hawaiians from their surveys in exchange for reducing expenses by not paying interviewers to work late into the night.

At any geographical level (national, state, or local), the effective population of interest for a poll typically will be more limited than all those residents who will vote. For example, since almost all preelection polling nowadays is done via telephone interviews, anyone who votes but does not live in a household with a telephone (less than 5 percent of American voters in the 1992 election) is excluded from the actual target population. Furthermore, anyone who does not speak a language in which the poll questionnaire has been written cannot be interviewed and is also technically omitted from the target population. But, once again, pollsters have learned that in almost all instances, restricting the population of interest to a more practical definition will not make an appreciable difference in the accuracy of their polls' projections of a likely winner or of the opinions of the American electorate.

What is a sampling frame?

Simply put, the *sampling frame* is a listing of the target population from which a sample is drawn. There is no standard list of all the registered voters in the United States that can be used by pollsters as a sampling frame for election polls, at least not one that is accurate and up to date and contains the telephone numbers of their residences.

In some cases, such a listing actually exists for a small subset of the population, somewhere physically on paper or in a computer file. When such a frame does exist, it can be used to draw a sample by selecting a portion of the voters or households from the list. For example, pollsters interested in doing a statewide poll in a state with a small population, such as North or South Dakota, might actually be able to assemble an entire listing of registered voters in the state to use as a sampling frame. Then they would have to associate the correct telephone numbers with the names and addresses of the registered voters. With currently available technology, this task would not be feasible in a large state or for the nation as a whole.

Do telephone directories make a good sampling frame for telephone surveys?

No, they usually do not. Many people are not represented in the telephone book because they do not have a telephone in their home or they do not have a listed number. For many, if not most, national election polls conducted in 1996, and for many others that will be conducted at the state and local levels, a different method will be used to assemble an appropriate sampling frame.

Telephone directories are rarely used as the sampling frame in modern election polls because a fairly large proportion of Americans have unlisted telephone numbers—numbers that are neither published in a telephone directory nor given out by directory assistance services. Current estimates are that approximately 35 percent of Americans live in telephone households without a listed telephone number. This varies greatly by state and by local region with Californians showing the greatest proclivity for not listing their telephone numbers; more than 60 percent of Californians with residential telephone service have unpublished or unlisted numbers.

Using telephone directories would not be a problem if research did not show that voters who do not list their telephone numbers are different from those who do. There are considerable differences between the voting behavior and intentions of those who list their telephone numbers in local directories and those who do not. For example, African Americans are much more likely, as a group, than are whites, as a group, to have an unlisted telephone number. Since African Americans, as a group, have historically been much more likely than others to vote for Democratic candidates, any election poll that used a telephone directory as its sampling frame would significantly underrepresent the African American vote. In most instances, such a poll would underrepresent the Democratic vote.

What is the sampling frame for a typical preelection telephone poll?

The sampling frame for a typical telephone poll is all residences that have phones. This is an "ideal" frame because no listing of such households actually exists. Therefore, pollsters have had to develop other methods to select the households to be called.

Instead of using directories as the sampling frame for telephone election polls, modern pollsters use a technique called *random-digit dialing* (RDD) to reach households with both listed and unlisted telephones. This sampling frame is not in fact an actual physical listing of all possible telephone numbers in a given geographical region. Instead, it is a frame that "theoretically" represents all the possible numbers. The random-digit dialing technique creates only a subset of all possible numbers—enough to complete the total number of interviews required by the sample design.

In random-digit dialing, a computer is used to choose telephone area codes that cover a given geographic region at random, and then the computer selects at random a three-digit telephone "prefix" that operates within that area code. Once these six digits have been chosen, the computer then adds four additional random digits to create a standard ten-digit telephone number.

This randomization process is repeated many hundreds or thousands of times, depending on the sample size desired for the election poll. Interviewers dial these randomly generated numbers to determine if each is working; and, if it is working, whether or not it is the number for a residence in which a potential voter can be interviewed. Currently, RDD is the preferred frame for most preelection polls that contact voters at their residences via telephone.

What is the sampling frame for the typical exit poll?

Exit polls are conducted via in-person interviews with citizens immediately after they have voted and are leaving their balloting places. These sample designs involve multiple stages at which different units are selected. The initial sampling frame is a "theoretical" listing of all possible voting places within the geographic region of interest. For national exit polls, the sampling frame starts with all 3,043 counties in the United States, and the design involves the random selection of a relatively small number. In the next stage, a random selection of voting precincts is drawn from a list of all of them in each selected county. In the third and final stage, a random sample of voters in each "sample precinct" is continuously drawn for interviews throughout the day and evening.

How large does a sample need to be?

Two important principles are associated with the size of a sample.

The first is that the larger the sample size, the more precise the estimate that can be made from it. People who design samples use the term *margin of error* to describe the precision of a sample estimate. This is a statistic that provides an estimate of the likely difference between a sample statistic and the actual or "true" value in the population.

All other things being equal, samples need to be as large as possible in order to produce as precise an estimate as possible. Another way that pollsters think about this issue is in terms of a reasonable sample size to produce a good estimate of the statistic they need. This consideration comes into play because the money saved by interviewing fewer people can often be used to increase the length of the interview itself or to improve quality control during the interviewing.

The second important principle is that the precision of a sample is not related to the size of the population from which it is drawn. In order to produce an estimate with a given margin of error, the same-size sample would have to be drawn from a city of 100,000, or a state with a population of 25 million people, or the entire United States, with its population of approximately 258 million residents.

What is the margin of error for a particular sample?

The larger a sample, the more precise is the estimate that can be produced from it. A larger sample produces a better estimate than a smaller sample, all other things being equal. The precision of a sample is described by its *sampling error,* or the margin of error around the estimate that it produces. The margin of error is a way of describing an interval in which the "true" value of the statistic for the entire population is likely to fall.

There are standard statistical formulas, originally developed for application to agricultural research, that can be used to determine how confident the pollster should be that a finding in the sample (e.g., the percentage who say they will vote for candidate X) reflects the target population's opinions or intentions on that measure. The *New York Times,* for example, always prints a methodology sidebar when reporting the results of its election polls. This sidebar explains the size of the poll's margin of error in language like the following:

> *In theory, in 19 cases out of 20, the results based on such samples (of 1,077 respondents) will differ by no more than three percentage points in either direction from what would have been obtained by seeking out all American adults.*[7]

Here, the newspaper is explaining that there is a degree of confidence (19 in 20, or 95 percent confidence)—not a certainty—that an estimate derived from the entire sample will approximate the same figure in the target population, ±3 percentage points.

Suppose a pollster conducts a survey to measure President Clinton's approval rating. In response to a specific survey question, 43 percent of those interviewed say they "approve" of the way Bill Clinton is handling his job as president. A sample of 1,500 respondents has a margin of error of 2.5 percentage points associated with it, at the 95 percent confidence level. That means that we can be reasonably confident (we can expect that 95 times out of 100) that President Clinton's approval rating lies between 40.5 percent (43 − 2.5 percent) and 45.5 percent (43 + 2.5 percent) in the population as a whole.

It is important to note that the margin of error does not get smaller in a direct fashion as the sample size increases. If one sample is twice as large as another, it will produce a margin of error that is only about 70 percent as great, not 50 percent as great.

How large does the sample size need to be?

That depends on how precise an estimate the pollster needs, in relation to how much money the organization or sponsor of the poll wants to spend for a probability sample. For most measures of public opinion, such as attitudes or intended voting behavior, a margin

7. *New York Times,* 26 October 1995, A11.

of sampling error of between 3 and 5 percentage points seems to be tolerable. That is, most issues do not produce opinions that are evenly divided (50–50), and analysts are confident that they can report that a majority favors one side or the other. Even in election analysis, most elections are not decided by margins of less than 52 to 48 percent, so a winner can safely be called in most cases with a margin of error of that magnitude.

On the other hand, if there were reason to believe that an election would be very close or that opinions were evenly divided on an issue, a polling organization might decide that a larger sample was needed to produce a more accurate estimate of the division of opinion or to indicate which side of an issue really had a majority of people supporting it.

Table 5.1 shows the margins of error associated with estimates produced from simple random samples of different sizes and for different confidence intervals.

As an aid in interpreting the table, the entries for samples of size 1,500 indicate that the margin of error due to chance alone would be ±2.5 percentage points for 95 out of 100 samples drawn. For a greater level of confidence (say, knowing that the sample estimate was within sampling error of the population value in 99 samples out of 100), the margin of error for the same-size sample

TABLE 5.1

MARGINS OF ERROR

Sample size	Tolerance at the 95% confidence level	Tolerance at the 99% confidence level
100	±9.8 percentage points	±12.9 percentage points
200	±6.9 percentage points	±8.2 percentage points
400	±4.9 percentage points	±6.5 percentage points
750	±3.6 percentage points	±4.7 percentage points
1,000	±3.1 percentage points	±4.1 percentage points
1,500	±2.5 percentage points	±3.3 percentage points
3,000	±1.8 percentage points	±2.4 percentage points
5,000	±1.4 percentage points	±1.8 percentage points

would of course be larger—approximately ±3.3 percentage points. If the sample size is doubled to 3,000 (that is, you spent about twice as much money collecting the data), the margin of error reduces to only ±1.8 percentage points.

If a preelection poll using a probability sample of about 1,100 voters finds that 45 percent intend to vote for candidate X, then the poll actually has found that somewhere between 42 and 48 percent of the target population will vote for candidate X. This range of 42 to 48 percent is technically referred to as a *confidence interval* around the population value; and the statistical procedures for calculating this "margin of sampling error" (3 percentage points in this example) will lead to a correct finding 95 percent of the time.

The table shows that there are very substantial reductions in the margin of error up to samples of about size 1,000. Beyond that, however, the improvements are less than 1 percentage point for reasonable increments in the sample size. For this reason, the typical media poll has a sample size between 1,000 and 1,500 respondents and rarely exceeds that because the cost of producing additional interviews does not significantly reduce the error due to chance alone.

Why are some sample designs preferable to others?

Sample designs differ in three ways. They need to be based on the laws of probability in order to take advantage of such concepts as the margin of error. They also vary in terms of the precision of the estimates they produce and the ease with which they can be implemented.

A probability design is one in which every unit in the population has a known, nonzero chance of being selected. If some units have no chance of being selected, or they can select themselves in, then this is not a probability design.

Some designs are less efficient than others, that is, they produce estimates with larger margins of error. Simple random samples generally have the smallest errors associated with them, but they are rarely used in election polls because there is no single list of registered voters, for example, that pollsters can use from which to select names at random. Pollsters have to construct a frame by using random-digit dialing techniques to select telephone households, for example, and then to select a respondent from among the eligible adults who reside there. There are different ways of going through this procedure, some of which are preferable to others. Generally, RDD samples have larger sampling errors than simple random samples.

What is a probability sample?

If a pollster selects voters from a sampling frame that represents the target population well and two additional conditions are met, then the poll has employed a form of probability sampling. These two necessary conditions are that (1) everyone in the sampling frame has a chance of being selected, and (2) the pollster can determine the actual probability of each person being selected. The value of probability samples is that they allow pollsters to use statistical formulas to determine how likely it is that the findings from the poll's sample accurately reflect the opinions and intentions of the target population with accuracy.

As indicated earlier, most preprimary and preelection polls will be conducted via telephone interviews. These polls are likely to use random-digit dialing (RDD) techniques to reach those households that contain the voters to be interviewed. Here, the target population is voters residing in households with telephones; the sampling frame is all possible household telephone numbers within the geographic area covered by the poll.

In order for an RDD sample to be a true probability sample, the pollster must know the probability of each household being reached and the probability that a given adult within the household was selected from all adults residing in that household. These are characteristics of households that change over time, representing changes in American lifestyles. Polling organizations must track these changes carefully and consistently in order to account for them in their sampling procedures.

For example, a household with two residential telephone lines has twice the chance of selection in the sample that a household with only one residential telephone number has. For more than twenty-five years, the number of lines per household was consistently only one, but that has changed in the past few years and will continue to change. By 1994, the proportion of households with more than one line had doubled to almost 16 percent. The beginning of this trend was in homes with teenagers, but the explosion primarily reflects people who work at home and the desire to access computerized information resources.[8] Therefore, the number of multiple-line households will continue to increase as access to the information superhighway becomes easier and cheaper.

Furthermore, people who live with several other adults (such as a husband and wife and their two adult live-in children) have a smaller probability of being selected within their own household as the designated respondent than those who live with no one else or just a few other adults. The average household size in the United States has actually decreased slightly in recent years, as a combination of an increased divorce rate and parents having fewer children.

Pollsters have to ask respondents to telephone surveys how many separate telephone numbers they have in their homes and how many other adults live in their homes in order to know how to calculate the probability of selection for each person who was interviewed. If pollsters cannot calculate these probabilities of selection, they cannot make proper use of the statistical formulas for calculating the survey's margin of error.

What is a nonprobability sample?

Any group of people can be polled and treated as a "sample." Unless pollsters use certain scientific techniques, however, they will have no way of knowing the extent to which the respondents' answers represent any definable larger population. Whenever a sample of voters is selected without regard to the target population they are supposed to represent, or the probabilities of selection are unknown, the pollster has employed some form of *nonprobability sampling*.

8. Mark Landler, "Multiple Family Phone Lines, a Post-Postwar U.S. Trend," *New York Times*, 26 December 1995, A1.

Strictly speaking, unless the pollster has formulated a sampling frame that represents the target population well and then uses some selection rule that gives everyone in the frame a nonzero chance of being selected, the pollster is using a *nonprobability sample.* If the pollster gives everyone in the sampling frame a chance of being selected but does not know the exact probability of selecting each person in the sampling frame, then once again the pollster is left with a nonprobability sample.

The disadvantage of a nonprobability sample is that pollsters cannot calculate a margin of error for the sample estimate and therefore cannot tell how accurately the sample represents the opinions or intentions of the target population. For example, market researchers often use a surveying technique referred to as *mall intercept interviews:* interviewers in a shopping mall stop a number of people and try to interview them. The findings from this type of nonprobability sample cannot be generalized to a target population because the researchers can neither accurately define what population is represented by the *intercept sample* nor the probability that each person in this unknowable population had of being selected. Election "straw polls" often use sampling techniques that resemble *mall intercept sampling.* There is no way to determine with any confidence the accuracy of an estimate of candidate preference derived from such straw polls in relation to the target population of persons who are likely to vote in the election.

Why are some samples preferable to others?

The purpose to which a poll's findings will be put should determine the sample design used. Whenever the pollster wants to produce an estimate that represents the intentions or opinions of a definable target population with a *known degree of confidence and accuracy* in the findings, a probability sample must be used.

But some polls are not meant to gather findings in order to describe the larger population with a known degree of accuracy. For example, in the early stages of the election season, a candidate's private pollster may want to study the opinions of a relatively rare group within the larger population—such as African American Republicans. The pollster (and the candidate) may not need to estimate how all African American Republican "likely voters" think about certain issues but may simply want to get a general sense of what issues appear to be of most concern to this group. The challenge here is to sample enough African American Republicans to meet this need.

One approach would be to use an unscientific *snowball sample* —one in which each African American Republican interviewed is subsequently asked to "nominate" others like himself, who will subsequently be contacted for an interview. This process continues until the sample "snowballs" to its desired sample size.

What is a random sample?

A sample can be drawn from a sampling frame in many ways. One common technique is called a *random sample* because the elements contained in the sampling frame are chosen at random. "At random" means that the choice of any one individual in the sampling frame is completely arbitrary and based on chance.

Sometimes a random sample is drawn with every person in the frame having an equal chance of being chosen. This is called an equal probability of selection method, or an *epsem sample.*

The main advantage of a random selection procedure is that it avoids any conscious or subconscious human bias from entering into the selection scheme. A *simple random sample* uses a set of "random numbers" that, nowadays, are typically generated directly from a computer program; formerly, they were selected from a "random numbers table" printed in statistics books (which were also generated at one time from a computer before they were typeset). The series of numbers consisting of 3, 47, 428, and 1,752 is a random series of numbers that, if applied to a sampling frame, would lead to the selection of the 3d, 47th, 428th, and 1,752d persons listed on the sampling frame.

Although it is unlikely to happen, a set of random numbers may yield an unrepresentative sample from the sampling frame. By "representative," we mean a sample that matches quite well the various demographic, behavioral, and attitudinal characteristics of the population of interest. For example, it is possible just by chance that a random set of selections could fall almost entirely within the first half of the sampling frame. If there were any order within the sampling frame, such as place of residence within the survey area, then these choices might be random, but not necessarily representative.

What is a systematic sample?

A *systematic sample* is a special form of random sampling. A systematic sample design *forces* the random selection to take place over the entire sampling frame, from the beginning through the end.

The way that this occurs is straightforward. First, a *sampling interval* is determined. The sampling interval is simply the total number of persons in the sampling frame divided by the number of persons to be sampled. If there are 1,000,000 persons in the sampling frame and the number to be sampled is 2,000, then the sampling interval would be 1,000,000/2,000, or 500. In this example, the next step in the sampling process involves choosing a *random start* between 1 and 500, say 322. Thus the 322d person on the sampling frame would be the first one selected. After that, every 500th person (822d; 1,322d; 1,822d; 2,322d; etc.) would be selected from the sampling frame. The last person to fall into the sample would be the 999,822d person on the list.

A systematic random sample has the advantages of being both random and more likely to be representative of the sampling frame, as long as the width of the sampling interval is in no way correlated with any peculiar pattern in the sample frame itself.

What is a stratified sample?

A *stratified sample* is another form of random sampling that strives to assure that the sample is also representative. Stratified sampling occurs when the sampling frame can be grouped into meaningful subcategories (*strata*), such as by gender or age or race or place of residence. Then either simple random sampling or systematic sampling procedures can be applied within each subgroup (*stratum*), assuring that a proportional number from each group gets chosen —something that will not necessarily occur with simple random sampling or systematic sampling. For example, if female voters are expected to constitute 55 percent of election turnout, then a sampling frame of registered voters could be stratified by gender and then 55 percent of the sample could be chosen from the female stratum.

Despite the advantages that stratified sampling affords pollsters who want to assure a random and representative sample, stratified sampling is often not feasible because not all lists can be grouped or organized according to meaningful strata.

Do you need a larger sample size with a national survey than you do in a statewide or citywide poll?

It comes as a big surprise to many people to learn that a sample size of 1,000 voters is no more accurate *from a sampling error standpoint* in measuring the voting intentions in a citywide election (in which the turnout will be several hundred thousand voters) than a sample of 1,000 voters in a national election that will have 110 million citizens going to vote. In this example, each poll's margin of error would be ±3 percentage points, with 95 percent confidence, if the elections were relatively close ones and there were not many undecided voters.

In most instances, polls intended to measure voting intentions among the electorate within a margin of error of ±3 percentage points will need approximately 1,000 to 2,000 voters, regardless of how many citizens will actually vote in the election. This rule begins to break down when the actual number of voters (the size of the target population) is small. In statistical terms, "small" begins to apply to target populations that are less than 10,000 in size. So, if a small-town election will have a turnout of 2,000 voters, for example, the margin of error for a preelection poll of 1,000 of those voters—half the voters—is in fact smaller than ±3 percentage points, as intuition might suggest. Even in this example, however, the margin of sampling error would decrease by only 1 percentage point to ±2 percentage points in a survey in which half the population of interest would be surveyed. This may defy logic, but nevertheless it is statistically accurate. Ultimately it all hinges on the role of "chance" and the less-than-total certainty a pollster has with anything other than a full census.

For most national preelection polls taken close to the November election day, the traditional sample size will be approximately 2,200 voters. This number is chosen because pollsters want to be able to predict the election outcome within ±2 percentage points. If pollsters for a statewide gubernatorial or senatorial election wanted the same level of accuracy, they too would need to survey about 2,200 voters across that state.

What is the response rate to a survey?

Every election poll conducted faces real fiscal limits and practical "timing" constraints. Polls must measure voters' opinions and intentions within a known and meaningful time frame. These limitations almost always lead to some people's being sampled for a poll but never interviewed.

The difference between the number of people sampled for a poll and the actual number interviewed is reflected in the poll's *response rate*. In its simplest form the response rate is the proportion of sampled voters who are eventually interviewed. For example, if 1,200 households were sampled for a telephone poll but only 800 interviews were completed during the poll's *field period*—the number of days, or even hours, that elapse from start to finish during which interviews are conducted—then the poll's response rate would be 800/1,200, or 67 percent. In this simple example, the size of the poll's *nonresponse rate* would be 33 percent, since one in three sampled households was not interviewed.

In most election polls, the pollster always has a predetermined sample size that needs to be achieved. The pollster then has interviewers contact "enough" sampled voters to reach the sample size. This process occurs because it is the sample size that typically drives the process, not the response rate. If a poll is conducted over a weekend, then the response rate will likely be much lower than if it were conducted over a longer time period, such as a week. This will happen because sampled people are harder to reach within a short field period (e.g., two days or less) than a longer field period (e.g., a week).

There are many reasons for nonresponse in polls, and thus for *low response rates;* but the primary problems that pollsters encounter are *noncontacts* and *refusals.* A noncontact occurs whenever a sampled household or person is never reached to be interviewed during the poll's field period. The busy lifestyles of members of the electorate and technologies such as answering machines have made it harder than it was as recently as two decades ago to contact sampled voters in telephone polls that have a short field period. Refusals too have become more frequent as many members of the public have come to feel hounded by telemarketers, market researchers, and pollsters—some of whom are unscrupulous in their methods and intents.

How does the response rate affect survey accuracy?

There are many possible threats to the accuracy of a survey. One of those is *nonresponse error,* which can occur in a poll if the group that is interviewed holds considerably different opinions and intentions from the group that was also sampled but not interviewed. Nonresponse is one of the major reasons that a sample of interviewed voters may not accurately represent or reflect the target population.

To explain how this works, imagine an election in which a young male challenger was running against an older female incumbent and both had fairly similar positions on issues. Suppose further that the female incumbent had been in office for several decades and the male challenger was running on the theme that "change is long overdue." If this theme were more attractive to younger voters, then nonresponse by people of a particular age range in a poll for this election contest could predictably lead to considerable error. Suppose a poll of 500, with a margin of sampling error of ±4 percentage points, showed the female incumbent with 54 percent support of those surveyed, with 46 percent support-ing the male challenger. Applying the poll's margin of error would lead to the conclusion that the incumbent would receive between 50 and 58 percent support and the challenger between 42 and 50 per-cent support. This looks like a close race, but with the incumbent expected to win.

If this poll were conducted via telephone over the weekend be-fore the election, it would not be unusual for the poll to achieve only a 50 percent response rate (or even less). Years of experience show that most telephone polls of voters find it much harder to reach younger adults, especially on weekends, than middle-aged and older adults. In this example, suppose the 50 percent of the sampled voters who were never interviewed supported the chal-lenger by a 60 percent to 40 percent margin. Here, the size of the nonresponse error would be calculated as follows: 46 percent of the 50 percent who *did* respond to the poll favored the challenger, and they represent 23 percent of the electorate who favor the challenger. To this would be added the 60 percent of the 50 percent who *did not* respond to the poll and who favor the challenger, or 30 percent. Thus the challenger would be expected to win this election with a (23 percent + 30 percent = 53 percent) majority of the vote. In other words, the analysis suggests that the first estimate that the chal-lenger would receive only 46 percent support had a nonresponse er-ror of 7 percentage points (53 percent − 46 percent)!

As explained in more detail in chapter 8, pollsters often try to reduce nonresponse error by making statistical corrections to their data in order to "adjust" for differences in their sample compared to their target population. These adjustments do not always work well, however. Unfortunately for pollsters and their clients, there is no way to know how well the adjustments worked until after the election.

Why have I never been interviewed in an election poll?

There are approximately 190 million adults in the United States who could conceivably be eligible to be sampled for an election poll. During the 1992 election season, a rough estimate suggests that more than 5,000 but fewer than 10,000 elections polls were conducted. Many of these were done by private pollsters who did not publicly release their results. If each of these polls contacted an average of 600 voters—most polls do not use sample sizes as large as 1,100 or 2,200—then in 1992 something like 3 to 4 million voters may have been interviewed or contacted by an election polling firm.

Thus, the chance that any one of the 190 million voters would have been contacted would only be somewhere between 1 in 45 (2.2 percent probability) and 1 in 60 (1.7 percent probability). Over the years, the probability for any one voter being contacted by an election poll would increase, but rather slowly, especially since it has only been in the past decade that we have experienced an "explosion" of election polling. So it really is not surprising that most Americans would say they have never been interviewed for an election poll.

But many more Americans have been sampled for an election poll than those that have been contacted, when nonresponse is taken into account. In fact, it is likely that at least three times as many Americans have been sampled for election polls compared to the number actually interviewed. Most of these voters are not aware that they were sampled because they were never at home at the time an interviewer tried to reach them.

References

HENRY, GARY T. 1990. *Practical Sampling.* Newbury Park, Calif.: Sage.
A highly readable primer on survey sampling that is part of a series on applied social research methods. This book is as an excellent "first read" for anyone who wants to become familiar with what survey sampling is all about, in a conceptual sense. It also provides an introduction to some more advanced issues in sampling and thus will benefit the reader who is planning to learn more about sampling.

Throughout the book, Henry stresses the differences between nonprobability samples and probability samples, noting that the weakness of all nonprobability samples is that the researcher cannot estimate the size of error (variance) associated with the sampling design and cannot know with confidence what target population is represented by the sample. The author explains the many different types of nonprobability samples and how they can benefit research as long as their limitations are recognized. These include convenience samples, "most similar/dissimilar" samples, "typical case" samples, "critical case" samples, "snowball" samples, and quota samples. The probability sampling techniques explained are simple random sampling, systematic sampling, stratified sampling, cluster sampling, and multistage sampling.

The book also makes explicit various cost/benefit sampling decisions that survey researchers face before, during, and after gathering data.

KISH, LESLIE. 1965. *Survey Sampling*. New York: Wiley.
The "bible" for advanced students and practitioners of survey sampling, this classic text remains important more than forty years after its first edition was published. Although the author intended it to be "a simple book on sampling methods," advanced statistical and methodological training is required before someone can comprehend and appreciate its depth and rigor.

The text goes into great detail, both statistically and methodologically, on many common types of samples, but concentrates mostly on the variety of probability samples. Sections are also included that deal with atypical sampling issues and problems such as area geographic sampling and sampling from "imperfect" frames. Anyone who has a detailed and specific need concerning survey sampling will be rewarded by taking the time to search for an answer in Kish.

SUDMAN, SEYMOUR. 1976. *Applied Sampling*. New York: Academic Press.
After twenty years, this remains a valuable resource for readers with some statistical background, both as an introduction to various aspects of sampling and as a somewhat advanced text. Many of the sections focus on the methods used to construct and implement various types of survey samples. Other sections detail the statistical underpinnings of sampling. A multitude of examples are used to illustrate the various sampling designs the book covers: simple random sampling, cluster sampling, stratified sampling, multistage sampling, and some nonprobability samples.

Sudman describes the book as "intended for researchers who have limited resources and statistical backgrounds and who wish to maximize the usefulness of the data they obtain." A primary purpose of the book is to provide instruction on how to make cost-effective decisions about sampling so that adequate data quality can be maintained. Sudman's goal is to empower everyday survey researchers with limited budgets and help them avoid sloppy sampling, thereby totally wasting their limited resources.

6

How Do Interviews
Take Place?

After a designated respondent has been selected in a household, the actual process of data collection begins. In most polls, this happens through a conversation when a trained interviewer asks the respondent a series of questions. There are several different ways in which this conversation can take place—on the telephone, face to face, or with the aid of a computer. In the case of exit polls, interviews are conducted by handing respondents a questionnaire and having them fill it out themselves.

Any of these *modes of data collection* can be used to gather data in scientific election polls, and some additional data-collection techniques are even used in unscientific "polls." In most of this century and in the last, the traditional mode for gathering election poll data has been to use interviewers who ask people questions "face to face." Nevertheless, interviewing people "in person" has also been used in the unscientific straw polls conducted by journalists, political campaign workers, and interested citizens in the United States as early as the mid-1800s.

Face-to-face questioning was the preferred interviewing method for many years because it was both practical and timely. It was practical in the sense that voters were often sampled and interviewed at their home addresses. And it was timely because, until recently, the media did not require immediate access to their poll findings in order to make news. In the past fifteen years or so, almost all polling has been done on the telephone.

What is the most common form of data collection in election polls?

Starting in the late 1970s, there was a shift to telephone interviewing as the preferred mode of data collection. By the early 1980s, virtually every preelection poll was conducted on the telephone. This shift came about as residential penetration of telephones exceeded 90 percent of all households by the end of the 1970s. At the same time, random-digit dialing (RDD) procedures were perfected as a sampling technique, allowing pollsters to reach households regardless of whether or not their numbers were listed. In combination, these factors affected the cost, timing, and quality of data that could be gathered via telephone in a way that they became as good, and often better, than what could be collected via face-to-face interviewing.

What other forms of data collection are there?

Scientific elections polls can also be gathered via *mail survey*. The costs of data collection by mail are low, but this is rarely done because valid mail surveys take much too long to complete in relation to other modes of data collection. A typical mail survey requires several weeks of elapsed time and multiple follow-up mailings in order to achieve an acceptable response rate. Without a good response rate, the poll is not likely to be a representative sample of the target population.

A new mode of scientific data collection, and one that will grow in usage, is *computer assisted personal interviewing* (CAPI), which incorporates the use of computers in self-administered surveying. It is not difficult to envision a time in the not-so-distant future when exit-poll interviewers will simply hand a voter a small computer, rather than a clipboard, to record their answers.

What are the advantages and disadvantages of face-to-face interviews?

Face-to-face interviewing evolved as the dominant mode of quality survey data collection at a time when there was little or no telephone service to most U.S. households. It is no longer the predominant mode of data collection because of its great cost. But it has some distinct advantages over the telephone and mail for data collection.

The main advantages of in-person interviewing are linked to the social realities of having the interviewer in the physical presence of the respondent. First, questionnaires can be much longer with face-to-face interviews than with the telephone interviews because neither the interviewer nor the respondent gets fatigued as quickly. It is not unusual for face-to-face interviews to take an hour or more, without seeming a burden to the respondent.

Second, more complicated question formats can be used in face-to-face interviews, including ones that employ visual aides as part of the questioning. Third, if a question requires respondents to "look up" an answer in their household records, they can be more easily persuaded to do this during a face-to-face interview in their home. Finally, an interviewer can unobtrusively and directly code information about the person, the home, and the neighborhood while visiting the location in which the interview takes place. This can be done without asking the respondent questions, as would be necessary on the telephone.

Apart from its relatively high cost, face-to-face interviewing has other disadvantages. Most important, there is the lack of constant interviewer supervision that is possible in a centralized telephone facility. Second, it is becoming increasingly difficult to find interviewers who are willing to go into certain neighborhoods and areas to poll because they are concerned about their personal safety. At the same time, respondents also are becoming less willing to let a "stranger" into their homes, even when the interviewer has ample identification and prior notification has been made that the interviewer will be arriving at a specific time on a specific day.

Unless there is a change in the legal and social climates that now make telephone interviewing the preferred and most cost-effective mode of data collection, there is no reason to expect a resurgence in the use of face-to-face interviewing for election polls. The one exception to this general rule is exit polling, where interviewers still travel to voting locations to sample and distribute self-administered questionnaires on clipboards. Even exit-polling procedures will come under review, however, as states modify voting procedures so that voters can cast their ballots early, as they can in Texas and Florida, or by mail, as they can in certain elections in sixteen different states.

What are the advantages and disadvantages of telephone interviews?

The primary advantages of the telephone as a data-collection mode are speed in obtaining data, ease of sampling target populations, and the opportunity to institute quality control over sampling and interviewing.

In terms of speed, a telephone poll can be conducted much quicker than a face-to-face survey because it is much easier to find respondents and to recontact hard-to-reach ones. It is only necessary to redial a telephone number, for example, rather than have an interviewer make a second trip to a home. Furthermore, the widespread usage of computer assisted telephone interviewing (CATI) procedures means that the data can be recorded simultaneously in a computer file as the interview takes place. Mail surveys suffer even greater time delays in gathering and processing the data.

The second advantage of telephone surveys is the relative ease of sampling. In the last decade, several companies have entered the business of supplying lists of telephone numbers to be used for polling. Some of these lists are directory based, and others incorporate random-digit dialing numbers as well. With about nineteen in twenty U.S. households having a telephone (and an even higher proportion among residences with "likely voters"), pollsters are not concerned about their inability to reach their target populations, providing they use the scientific methods that are readily available. Unlike face-to-face or mail surveys that sample addresses, a researcher using a telephone survey immediately learns if a telephone number is no longer in service. The researcher does not have to wait to learn that an interviewer went to a home only to find out that the residents have moved or that a mailed questionnaire has come back marked "return to sender" because a different person lives at the address or the intended respondent has moved.

The third major advantage of telephone surveys is one that too often is not realized. Even though telephone interviewing has become the dominant mode for conducting preelection polls, it is surprising how few polling organizations take full advantage of its considerable opportunities to improve the quality of data. As with many things, this comes down to the issue of cost—it costs more to do things better! Yet many polling organizations do not appear to understand that a little more investment of resources can yield big payoffs in data quality when using the telephone as the mode of data collection. To achieve this enhanced level of quality, a telephone facility must be structured to promote *standardized survey interviewing*, with the constant interaction of skilled supervisors helping their teams of trained interviewers strive for the ideal of data without any interviewer-related errors.

A fourth advantage concerns the safety of interviewers who do not need to travel anywhere. Sometimes this also works as an advantage for respondents who do not want to admit an interviewer into their homes.

What are the advantages and disadvantages of self-administered questionnaires?

A poll that uses a self-administered questionnaire can achieve a good response rate and have some significant advantages over face-to-face and telephone polling. The most important features are the privacy with which respondents can participate. In mail surveys, a common mode of data collection with self-administered questionnaires, many respondents find it more convenient to schedule when they will complete the questionnaire. This also gives them time to think about their answers to the questions. And pollsters have the possibility of including visual aids as a supplement to complicated question formats. Respondents also find it easier to "look up" information without feeling rushed by the interviewer.

Another advantage of mail surveys is their relatively low cost. It actually costs much more to conduct a valid mail survey of the public than most people realize, because of the need to do several follow-up mailings to achieve a good response rate. But these costs are still substantially lower than face-to-face interviews and generally lower than telephone interviews as well. Mail surveys also afford respondents the opportunity to retain their anonymity, instead of merely receiving a pledge of confidentiality from an interviewer. This is a complex issue because devising a mail survey that provides true anonymity precludes the use of many techniques that are usually needed to raise otherwise low response rates.

There are also many disadvantages associated with self-administered questionnaires. If sample selection procedures allow respondents to make the decision about whether or not they will participate in a poll, then serious self-selection biases can result. This is what happens too often with mail surveys and other forms of self-administered questionnaires. Although low response rates can be overcome if a mail survey is well conceptualized and well implemented, nonresponse remains the bane of many mail polls. In part because of the added time required for follow-up mailings, many pollsters forgo additional mailings to increase their response rates because their client's deadlines do not allow time for follow-up mailings.

Another significant disadvantage of mail surveys is the "timing" necessary to conduct them. This is the most common reason for ruling out a mail survey with a self-administered questionnaire as the data-collection mode for an election poll. It simply takes much too long to conduct a valid mail poll for the needs of the news media and of most private poll sponsors, such as candidates.

From the perspective of the resulting data themselves, self-administered questionnaires sometimes produce incomplete or ambiguous answers that cannot be clarified in the way they could if an interviewer were present. Therefore, there is often a good deal more "missing" and "unusable" data in a mail survey than one that is conducted in person by interviewers.

There are some new developments on the horizon in the use

of self-administered questionnaires. Some pollsters are looking to use the Internet as a mode for sending out self-administered surveys and getting back quick responses. Samples based on respondents who own computers and have access to the Internet can present substantial problems of representativeness of the population as a whole. It will not be possible in 1996 to reach a representative sample of U.S. voters by this method, and readers should beware of any "findings" from such polls, as they most assuredly will be invalid. But the possibilities of computerized surveying will increase as the availability of home computers increases, just as the penetration of telephones altered the standard means of data collection prior to the 1970s.

In another development, self-administered questionnaires are starting to be used in studies where a respondent is brought to a research office and uses a computer to complete the questionnaire. To our knowledge, this is not a technique that will be used for 1996 election polling. Nevertheless, we can envision a time in the not-too-distant future when computers will be brought to respondents —at their homes or at voting locations—to allow them to complete self-administered questionnaires.

What are some of the unscientific modes of data collection?

Some data-collection techniques used in "polls" are unscientific. When we speak of unscientific polls, we mean that the people who conduct them have no way of knowing whether the resulting data are an accurate reflection of the population they are supposed to represent. These include audience "call-in" polls in which a few telephone numbers are publicized for viewers, listeners, or readers to call to register their opinions on an issue. As discussed in greater detail in chapter 10, these data-collection techniques are both simplistic and completely unreliable. The same criticism holds for "polls" inserted in newspapers and magazines. Their primary purpose is to build interest and loyalty among readers by soliciting their views on current affairs or issues of the day.

Another form of unreliable polling involves the use of sophisticated telecommunications equipment, often employing advanced voice-detection capabilities. In these ventures, a computer can be programmed to dial telephone numbers. The person who picks up the phone hears a series of questions read by an audio recording. Sometimes these endeavors get celebrities to record the questions in order to make the listeners think this famous person actually cares what they think about the issues. The system can detect when a person has finished answering a question (has stopped talking) and then it plays the next question. Sometimes, instead of using voice detection, the computerized recorded voice tells respondents which touch-tone key number on the telephone to push to indicate a response to the question ("Push '1' if you agree").

Who gets to be an interviewer?

When they conduct face-to-face and telephone surveys, polling organizations employ interviewers to gather the data from respondents. In order to collect reliable and valid data, these interviewers must be skilled, well trained, and well supervised.

Quality polling operations recruit and train adult interviewers of all ages, genders, and ethnic and racial backgrounds. Extensive research has shown that the demographics of skilled interviewers are generally unrelated to the data they elicit from respondents with the exception of surveys that ask substantive questions about topics such as gender issues, race relations, and the like. In these cases, the demographics of the interviewer and the respondent *may* interact in ways that can unintentionally bias the data. In some polls that measure the "gender gap," for example, male interviewers may elicit consistently different answers from male respondents than female interviewers do.

During the recruitment process, polling organizations look for interviewers having a pleasant voice with ample volume. Interviewers should speak neither too quickly nor too slowly, and they should project confidence when speaking to a stranger (the respondent). These are just general guidelines, as there is a tremendous range of variation in the voices of successful interviewers.

How are interviewers trained?

Skilled interviewers must be trained to read questions exactly as they are worded. They also have to learn to use *nondirective probing* to follow up responses to open-end questions and ambiguous responses to closed-end questions. Nondirective probing takes place when an interviewer encourages a respondent to answer a question more fully, but does so in a manner that is neutral and does not bias the response itself.

Polling organizations concerned about the quality of their work provide careful supervision of their interviewers. Telephone interviewers work in a centralized facility and not at home, so supervisory personnel can closely monitor interviewers and provide constant feedback and on-the-job training. In many organizations, supervisors routinely monitor ongoing telephone interviews in a manner that is unobtrusive to both the interviewer and respondent in order to gain a "real time" assessment of interviewers' work. Despite what many think, this monitoring is not illegal because it is done for training purposes and not to learn anything about a particular respondent. Nevertheless, it is a courtesy to respondents to have interviewers inform them that monitoring might occur while the interview is being conducted.

How does contact with a respondent take place?

The initial contact with most respondents typically occurs in their homes. The interviewer begins the contact by using an *introductory statement* that the pollster has crafted to introduce the interviewer and the survey, briefly explain its purpose, and help gain the cooperation of the person within the household who is to be interviewed. The importance of this latter point—gaining cooperation of the *designated respondent*—is often not understood or appreciated by people who are not researchers. If a survey does not use a systematic respondent selection technique to select one person from within each household to interview, then biases in the poll data are likely to result. This could take the form of interviewing too many women and older adults to get a representative sample of the target population. Furthermore, if the wording of the introduction does not induce respondent cooperation, then many will refuse. A low response rate can have disastrous consequences for a poll's accuracy.

The goal of most introductory sequences is to provide a minimum, yet adequate, amount of information about the study for the respondent to make a reasonably informed decision about whether or not to participate. The statement cannot provide too much information about the study because it could bias subsequent responses to the questions. But it has to provide enough information to engage a respondent's interest in continuing.

Polling organizations that strive for high-quality data collection will provide their interviewers with extensive "fall back" material to help them explain more about the poll if a curious or reluctant respondent needs such information. For example, in random-digit dialing polls some respondents with unlisted telephone numbers ask, "How did you get my number?" Interviewers must be able to provide a brief, informative, easily understood, and honest response to that question, and they should be trained to do so with skill.

Ethical polling requires that respondents understand that their participation in a survey is voluntary, and their responses will be held in total confidence and reported only after being aggregated with the responses of the other respondents for statistical analysis. The purpose of this assurance is to make it clear that no harm will come to them, whether or not they choose to participate in the survey.

How long does an interview take?

The length of time a respondent can expect to be interviewed in the typical election poll conducted on the telephone will generally range between ten and thirty minutes, although there will be a good deal of variation among respondents in the same poll. An interview of this length will generally consist of somewhere between 50 and 150 closed-end questions. The purpose of the poll and the amount of funding it has available will determine how lengthy a questionnaire can and will be used. Polls shorter than ten minutes are uncommon because a significant portion of polling costs involves the effort made to contact respondents and gain their cooperation. Once contact is made, there is little cost-savings incentive to avoid asking upward of fifty questions or so because each additional question can be asked for a relatively small marginal cost. Including the many demographic and political background questions that will be asked in most polls, it is surprising how quickly a questionnaire will fill up with items that need to be asked for the poll's main purpose. Using a telephone questionnaire that takes longer than thirty minutes also is uncommon because response rates generally decline with these relatively lengthy questionnaires, as respondents tire and break off the interview. It is also true that the quality of answers suffers in the last parts of a long interview.

The initial contact an interviewer makes to explain the survey and elicit the cooperation of the designated respondent often takes less than one minute. After the interview begins, the time it takes to administer the questionnaire will vary across respondents by a factor of about two; that is, the fastest interviewers and respondents, working together, will take about half as much time to go through an interview as the slowest pairs.

Another factor that affects the time it takes for an individual respondent to be interviewed will be the number of "contingency" question sequences the questionnaire contains—that is, linked questions that are not asked of everyone because they do not apply—and how many of these sequences an individual respondent's answers will invoke. In the case of a questionnaire that has several contingency sequences, respondents whose pattern of answers causes them to be "skipped out" of each linked sequence will complete the questionnaire much sooner than those whose answers invoke all the linked sequences.

The reader may find it interesting to learn that follow-up research with poll participants shows that most of them significantly *underestimate* the time it took for them to complete the interview. It is probably an overstatement to invoke the saying that "time flies when you are having fun" to explain this phenomenon, but many election poll respondents do enjoy having their opinions taken when done by a competent polling organization.

Interviews conducted face to face generally take longer to complete than telephone interviews. This is thought to reflect, in part, the social courtesies of not rushing when one is in the physical presence of another human; on the telephone, this norm does not seem as relevant.

It also may surprise the reader to learn that experience with computer-assisted interviewing in the past decade has shown that it takes approximately 20 percent *longer* to ask a series of questions in this mode than to ask the same questions as a *paper-and-pencil interview* (PAPI). This appears to be related to the fact that an interviewer has more direct control of the pace of questioning when using paper and pencil than when using a computer. On the computer, a subsequent question comes onto the screen only after the previous response has been recorded. With paper and pencil, the interviewer often starts reading the next question on the page while recording the answer to the previous question. Of course, this leads to some coding errors in paper-and-pencil interviewing that do not occur with computer-assisted interviewing.

Can interviewers affect the kinds of answers respondents give?

Quality pollsters strive to employ interviewers who have the skills and the willingness to engage in *standardized survey interviewing*.

Simply put, standard survey interviewing refers to interviewers who read questions exactly as written—thus exposing all respondents to the same stimulus (the same question wording). These procedures also include following up incomplete or ambiguous responses with *nondirective probes*—probes that merely encourage a fuller response instead of conveying to respondents that they are giving a "right" or "wrong" answer. The best pollsters also strive to create a work environment that will promote this ideal behavior in their data-collection staff.

Interviewers are human, however, and even the best will unintentionally, yet nonetheless occasionally, contribute "error" to the data they gather. Given that many polls are conducted by interviewing staffs that are neither well trained nor well supervised, it is probably the case that a good deal of error in polls is caused by interviewer-related behavior.

Two examples illustrate how this happens. First, interviewers might unconsciously and unintentionally reinforce certain types of answers that a respondent gives later in a questionnaire by making positive comments ("Oh, that's good") after some answers and negative comments ("Oh, that sounds bad") after other answers. Second, interviewers may let their own politics contaminate the way they read a question, conveying with their voice that they expect a certain "correct" answer to an opinion question. Accurate measurement of public opinion using polls depends on respondents believing that there are no "right" or "wrong" opinions, at least not as far as the pollster and the interviewers are concerned.

Anyone who participates in an election poll and encounters an interviewer who appears to be poorly trained or biased should ask to speak to the interviewer's supervisor or consider contacting the polling organization. The supervisor and pollster should thank any respondent who brings these kinds of problems to their attention because correcting them will improve the quality of the data.

What happens if initial contact is unsuccessful?

As discussed in chapter 5, survey nonresponse occurs whenever an interview is not obtained from a sampled household or designated respondent. The primary causes of nonresponse are never contacting people who fall in the sample at a time when they are available to be interviewed or having the sampled person refuse to participate. In order to lessen the chance that nonresponse will contribute to the inaccuracy of the poll—which can happen whenever nonrespondents as a group hold significantly different opinions and intentions than the respondents—a good polling organization will work hard to reduce nonresponse in their surveys.

The simplest way to reduce this potential problem of *non-*

contacts is to have interviewers try and try again, at different times of the day and different days of the week, to reach the respondent at a convenient time. It is not unusual for academic surveys to try to reach a sampled individual ten or more times before giving up. Most media polls must be completed within a field period of two or three days, however, making it very difficult to reach many of the sampled people because only one or two callback attempts are feasible. Experience shows that males and younger adults are the hardest respondents to reach in polls with brief field periods.

To reduce the potential problem of *refusals*, pollsters sometimes have a group of especially talented interviewers who try to "convert" people who told a previous caller that they would not participate in the survey. Sometimes the original refusal occurred because the interviewer called at an inconvenient time, when a person was working around the house or engaged in an activity he or she did not want to interrupt. These people were indisposed to be interviewed when first called, but they may have the time when called a second or third time. Once again, this process may be impractical in many media polls, where the field period extends only over a few days. In surveys with longer field periods, refusal conversions can yield somewhere between a 25 to 40 percent success rate; that is, one-fourth or more of initial refusals eventually can be converted to completed interviews. Experience shows that initial refusals are more likely to come from women and older adults, but these are also the two demographic subgroups who are most likely subsequently to agree to an interview when skilled refusal-conversion interviewers recontact them.

One method that scientific surveys do not use to compensate for cases of noncontact or refusals is to "replace," or substitute another household or person for the one sampled originally. Sampling with replacement can create serious problems of bias in the results if people who refuse to participate or cannot be located are systematically different from those who do respond, and they are replaced by more willing respondents. Poorer-quality polling organizations may employ this substitution approach, but only with serious risk.

How does information from a respondent get recorded in a computer?

The process of data gathering in a poll is motivated by an interest in having data to analyze in order to answer a research question. Poll data are analyzed with computers using statistical software. In order to analyze the data, the answers that respondents provide are almost always represented as numbers on the questionnaire and in a data file. These numerical data files are what pollsters analyze to determine the poll's results.

The traditional way that respondents' answers were entered into a computer-friendly form was to have them transferred from paper (the printed questionnaire) to a computer file by *data entry* workers. Until the past decade this was still mostly done by *key punching* the numbers onto computer cards, which in turn were "read" into a computer by various means. Nowadays, when a poll is taken via a paper-and-pencil questionnaire, the data are transferred directly into a computer file. Yet even this process is used less frequently in most telephone polls because of the widespread adoption of computer assisted telephone interviewing (CATI) software that allows data entry simultaneously with the interviewing process. The changes in computer technology in the past two decades have radically improved the speed at which polls can be analyzed, as well as the accuracy of the data, because there is less likelihood of human error in the data entry process.

In addition to recording and analyzing the responses given to closed-end questions—which typically are precoded with numeric values such as Yes = 1, No = 2, and Uncertain = 9—many polls gather responses to open-end items in which the respondent's own words are the "answers." These *verbatim responses* must be coded and transcribed into meaningful and reliably quantified categories before they can be analyzed. This is a labor-intensive venture, since reliable coding categories must first be devised, coders have to be trained to use the categories accurately, and reliability checks of the coders' work should be conducted. If the pollster's client simply wants to use the respondents' verbatims as interesting quotes, then this costly coding process is unnecessary.

Do respondents have to give their names when they are interviewed?

The short form of the answer to this question is no, but there are some instances in which respondents might want to consider giving their names and other contact information to an interviewer.

If a pollster knows someone's name, it means the poll is not anonymous. But the polling organization should nonetheless guarantee confidentiality by pledging that the data a respondent provides will not be released to anyone except in aggregated form where all answers are pooled together and summarized in statistical tables or figures. In this way, no one person's identity can be linked to his or her responses.

There are several reasons why a polling organization might want to be able to recontact a respondent. Pollsters may want someone's name if the client would like to reinterview the respondent at some later time. In some media polls, contact information is requested so that a reporter may call back to talk to a respondent at greater length about his or her views. This respondent could even end up being quoted by name (and with a photograph) in a subsequent newspaper story. The interviewer will usually have given each respondent a pledge of confidentiality at the beginning of the interview, so respondents will have to be asked to waive this guarantee before giving their names or addresses.

Respondents should understand that the polling organization knew something about their household before the interview began. A sample for a mail survey is based on a list of names and addresses. In face-to-face polling at a person's home, the interviewer will always know the address of the home, but not necessarily the household's or respondent's name, unless it is asked and given. In telephone polls that use random-digit dialing, the name of the household is never known unless it is asked and given, or unless the telephone number is a listed number and the pollster later uses a telephone number database to cross-check the numbers of households in which interviews were completed against those listed in the database. Polls that sample individuals from voter registration lists, whether conducted by mail, in person, or via telephone, will know the sampled respondent's name in advance, and the questionnaire will either be addressed to that person or the interviewer will ask to speak with that person (and no one else).

Nevertheless, you do want to be concerned if a private "poll" is really a fund-raising gimmick or a way to construct a mailing list for a subsequent sales pitch. And you do not have to supply any personal information that might be used for such purposes.

If you are contacted and asked to participate in an election poll, it is only prudent to think at least briefly about whether the pollster is likely to know your name and, if so, whether you should have any reasonable concern about this. We can neither automatically encourage everyone to release their names to pollsters nor discourage everyone from doing so. We do encourage readers to use common sense in deciding whether or not they should give out their names if they are asked in an election poll. Here, a good rule of thumb is: if you are uncertain, ask the interviewer to clarify *why* your name is being requested. If you are mailed a questionnaire and it asks for identifying information, you may want to contact the polling organization to ask about this. If you do give your name, make certain you understand whether or not you also are waiving your rights to have your responses kept confidential.

References

DILLMAN, DONALD A. 1978. *Mail and Telephone Surveys: The Total Design Method.* New York: Wiley.
The most widely respected book written to date about the "practice" or application of survey research methods. This is very much a "how to do a survey" book via mail or telephone. Although it is somewhat dated, having been written nearly two decades ago, its comprehensive, detailed, logical approach to doing surveys shows the thinking that one still should go through to attend to all aspects of survey quality and to achieve the best possible data for the finite resources available. Dillman based his development of the Total Design Method on a social exchange theory of why people do and do not respond to questionnaires.

The book provides step-by-step instruction on how to determine what mode of data collection to use, how to choose the best sampling design for the mode chosen, how to write survey questions, and how to lay them out for a mail survey or for a telephone survey questionnaire. The implementation of both mail and telephone surveys are also discussed in great detail, including how to construct an effective cover letter, what to include in the package that is mailed to a respondent, when and how to do follow-up mailings, the best methods for selecting respondents within households, how to recruit and train interviewers, and many other mundane but nevertheless very important aspects of high-quality surveying.

FOWLER, FLOYD J., JR., AND THOMAS W. MANGIONE. 1990. *Standardized Survey Interviewing*. Newbury Park, Calif.: Sage.
This brief but highly focused volume is part of a series on applied social research methods. It focuses entirely on the role of the interviewer in face-to-face and telephone surveys and on the error that can be contributed by the behavior of survey interviewers. This is an invaluable book for anyone who needs to understand how interviewers can help or hurt survey data quality, and it provides many ideas about how to minimize interviewer-related survey error.

The authors begin by defining standardized survey interviewing, explaining what this means in terms of discrete behaviors that interviewers must be trained to exhibit. The core of this standardized approach includes reading questions as they are worded, using nonbiasing probes on inadequate answers, accurately recording answers, being interpersonally neutral, and "training" the respondent so that the most accurate data are provided as responses to the questions asked.

The book provides a great deal of practical instruction about how the questionnaire can be constructed to help the interviewer maintain as close to "error free" behavior as is reasonably possible. Throughout the book, the authors cite their own and others' research on interviewing quality to explain and supplement the points being made. Especially valuable sections include the ones on the effects of interviewer characteristics, interviewer training, and supervision.

GROVES, ROBERT M. 1989. *Survey Errors and Survey Costs*. New York: Wiley.
Probably the most important and most comprehensive book to date on understanding the strengths and limitations of survey research methods. A demanding text that is required reading for all advanced students and practitioners of survey methods.

This challenging compendium provides a critical organization, review, and elaboration of past thinking on various weaknesses in sample surveys, each of which can be a source of error in survey estimates. The book "consolidates information from the literature on survey errors from both social science and statistics, drawing on the statistical sciences for insights into measuring the errors and on the social sciences to explain why they exist."

Groves explains in detail the differences between coverage error, nonresponse error, sampling error, and measurement error. All along he makes it clear that within the finite resources that survey practitioners constantly face, many difficult cost-benefit tradeoffs must be made in order to attain the best possible—most likely to be accurate—survey findings. The book also makes constant reference to the difference between survey methods that might reduce the size of potential sources of error versus methods that might yield important information about the nature and size of various errors.

LAVRAKAS, PAUL J. 1993. *Telephone Survey Methods: Sampling, Selection, and Supervision.* 2d ed. Newbury Park, Calif.: Sage.
A book in a series on applied social research methods that focuses entirely on various stages of data collection in telephone surveys. As virtually every election poll is conducted on the telephone, this book provides a detailed explanation of the methods and procedures that must be used to gather valid data. The book explains how telephone samples are created, with special concentration on various random-digit dialing schemes, the type that are most commonly used in preelection polls. The processes are detailed with an eye toward decreasing survey nonresponse and avoiding possible coverage errors. Securing the cooperation of a respondent is explained, and several within-housing-unit selection methods are illustrated. Considerable attention is given to issues of recruiting, hiring, and training interviewers. The findings from the author's own research are used throughout the text.

The organizing theme for the sections is the "total survey error" perspective. The book explains to the reader the many ways that survey accuracy might be increased, noting the ways that each method will have its own cost-benefit tradeoffs. Wherever relevant, the book makes note of the important practical difference between telephone surveys conducted via computer and those conducted by traditional paper-and-pencil methods.

7

HOW ARE QUESTIONNAIRES
PUT TOGETHER?

The questionnaire is the main data-collection device in a poll or survey. You can think of it as the "vehicle" for gathering information from survey respondents. It serves the same function that an electron microscope does for a biochemist or a powerful telescope for an astronomer. For this reason, many survey researchers refer to the questionnaire as the *instrument*.

Each questionnaire consists of a number of questions. These are the specific tools that pollsters use to take their measurements. Regardless of whether people are surveyed via mail, telephone, or in person, it is the individual survey question that is the source of the data that pollsters later analyze.

Pollsters often refer to these questions as the *items* in a questionnaire. Election poll questionnaires typically include items that measure people's opinions; knowledge of candidates and issues; voting intentions in forthcoming primaries or elections; whether and how they voted in past elections; and background demographics such as gender, age, education, and party identification.

The quality of the data collected in a poll can be a function of which questions are asked, how the individual questions are worded, how the respondent is allowed to answer to the questions, and even the order in which they are asked. The details of these issues and the results of some research on their effects is summarized in the answers to the following questions.

Does a questionnaire follow a particular format?

At a certain level, it does. You can think of a questionnaire as a *script* for a *conversation* between an interviewer and a respondent. The conversation generally begins with a set of opening items that are friendly and not too taxing for the respondent. This occurs for two reasons: the interviewer can put the respondent at ease and establish some rapport with him or her, and the respondent will not be likely to terminate the interview.

Do different survey questions serve different purposes?

Yes, there are many different purposes for survey questions, and their use depends on the information the pollster wants to collect. Some questions might serve a single purpose, while other questions might serve multiple purposes.

Some survey questions are formulated so the pollster can simply *describe* what is occurring in the electorate at the time the poll is taken. For example, asking the question, "Do you approve or disapprove of the way the president is handling the economy?" allows the pollster to report, in a descriptive fashion, the percentage of the public that "approves," the percentage that "disapproves," and the percentage that is "undecided" at the time the poll was conducted.

Other questions are used because they allow the pollster both to *describe* and to *predict* specific opinions or behaviors in the electorate. For example, a pollster might survey citizens in one state and measure their opinions about a political issue such as gun control. The pollster will look for correlations between the respondents' demographic characteristics and their attitudes toward the issue. If there are statistically significant correlations, the pollster can develop a formula or a model to predict attitudes toward gun control using the demographics. As a result, the pollster might then be able to predict the gun-control attitudes of unsampled citizens in another state, just by knowing the demographic characteristics of the population in that other state.

Still other questions are asked because they allow the pollster to *describe, predict,* and *explain why* something might happen or might have happened. Take the case of a pollster working for a political candidate who conducts a survey to help the candidate's campaign staff plan their future advertising. All the respondents are asked to evaluate the candidates near the beginning of the questionnaire. Then the sample is randomly divided into two halves.

The first half of the respondents are prompted with some "positive" information about the candidate, and the pollster remeasures the respondents' opinions of the candidate and the opponent. The other random half of respondents are prompted with "negative" information about the candidate's opponent, and their opinions of the candidate and the opponent are remeasured. If the favorability ratings of the candidate and the opponent change under the two different promptings, the pollster would have found something to explain the positive/negative differences, at least to a certain degree. This type of "cause and effect" research could be very useful in planning the campaign's future ads.

Is there more than one kind of survey question?

Yes, there are many different kinds of survey questions. A basic distinction among question types is whether or not the item provides a respondent with a fixed set of answers to choose from—what pollsters call *response alternatives*—or the respondent is allowed to answer in his or her own words and phrases.

When respondents are allowed to answer a question in their own words, the survey item is called an *open-end* question. An example of a common open-end question is:

> *What do you think is the most important problem facing the country today?*

In contrast, when respondents are presented with a group of answers to choose from, the item is called a *closed-end* question. An example of a closed-end question is:

> *Do you strongly agree, agree, disagree, or strongly disagree that the*

United States should send troops to support NATO's mission in Bosnia?

Other times, respondents might be asked a question, given several response choices, and then asked to pick "all that apply." This is a special form of closed-end question that provides for multiple responses. For example:

Which of the following is a reason why you intend to vote for Senator Dole? Strong Character; Good Policies; Identify with Senator's Political Party; Don't Like the Opponent? Please tell me all of these reasons that apply to you.

Since *open-end questions* allow respondents to use their own words to express a complex answer, the resulting data are usually thought to be a more valid reflection of their attitudes than when restrictions are placed on the range of possible answers by forcing a choice among a predetermined set of alternatives.

But a problem with open-end questions is that their answers must be coded (transformed) into meaningful categories before the pollster can make analytic sense of them. This coding process is labor intensive and therefore expensive and time-consuming. Furthermore, it is sometimes difficult to code such responses accurately.

Closed-end questions provide a range of responses that can make some respondents feel constrained in their ability to answer. A set of closed-end response categories for an item must be both "exhaustive" (each possible answer should fit into one of the response categories) and "mutually exclusive" (all possible answers should fit into *only one* of the response categories).

Closed-end questions sometimes create difficulties for pollsters because they offer a somewhat artificial and simplistic range of choices for an item. Some respondents find it frustrating to have to answer a question in the pollster's terms rather than in their own words.

Are there other differences between open-end and closed-end questions?

In addition to the response alternatives they offer, the process by which the answers (the data) are taken from respondents differs by type of question. For polls conducted over the telephone or in person, closed-end questions are easier for interviewers to ask. They simply read the item and its response alternatives and then they mark the choice corresponding to the respondent's answer. If the respondent is unclear or seems unable to give an immediate answer, the well-trained interviewer simply repeats the closed-end item and its choices, reading exactly what the pollster has written.

In open-end items, interviewers often have to "prompt" respondents to get them to answer more fully. Here the challenge is for the interviewer to do this in a "nondirective" fashion, that is, by using words that will not bias the answer the respondent will provide. Often, this is not very easily done. Furthermore, the *verbatim responses* recorded by interviewers sometimes are very difficult to read if they are handwritten and/or contain poor spelling.

In self-administered questionnaires, such as those used in *mail surveys,* respondents have to "work harder" to answer open-end items than closed-end items. For the latter, the respondent simply has to mark a choice. For the former, the respondent must write out the answer either by printing or in longhand. To some extent, this *respondent burden* can reduce the frequency of responses to particular questions, so the poll is likely to suffer from incomplete or at least abbreviated answers to some questions—answers that would have been prompted for greater detail if an interviewer had been administering the item. Legibility of handwriting can also be a problem when open-end items are gathered in self-administered polls.

What is an unbalanced question?

Poll questions also can vary in terms of whether they are *balanced* or *unbalanced.* This attribute generally refers to the continuum of the response alternatives that are offered in closed-end items.

A balanced question is constructed so that it equally represents both sides of an issue and provides the respondent with a scaled set of response alternatives that has a conceptual midpoint. Balanced questions are worded to make explicit two (or more) sides of an issue. For example, "Some people agree with the president that U.S. troops should be sent to Bosnia, while other people disagree," would be balanced wording for use at the start of a poll item measuring a respondent's own opinion about sending troops to Bosnia. If the item had been worded with only the first part of this phrasing, "Some people agree with the president that U.S. troops should be sent to Bosnia," leaving out the explicit phrasing that there are others who disagree, this would be unbalanced wording. Questions with unbalanced wording, apart from their response alternatives, often bias the answers that respondents give.

As an example of an unbalanced set of response alternatives, consider the prospect of a respondent's agreement with a candidate's position on an issue when offered "strongly agree," "agree somewhat," and "disagree" as choices. These alternatives are unbalanced because there is no conceptual midpoint within the set of responses. A balanced version of the response alternatives would include something like "strongly agree," "agree somewhat," "disagree somewhat," and "strongly disagree." Here the conceptual midpoint is located between the two "somewhat" responses and the response alternatives are balanced on both sides of the conceptual midpoint.

The reader should note that the midpoint in this example is not represented by an actual response choice. Some questions would offer a true midpoint, such as "neither agree nor disagree." Whether or not a set of responses is balanced or unbalanced does not necessarily suggest that it will bias respondents' answers. Nevertheless, a balanced question offers a respondent a set of symmetrical response alternatives from which to choose and does not suggest that there is a "preferred" answer to the question.

Does the wording of a question make a difference in the responses the interviewer receives?

It most assuredly does! Even small variations in wording and grammar may represent completely different questions to respondents. Although slight wording differences do not necessarily represent different concepts, small variations can lead to significant differences in the responses elicited. Unfortunately, the pollster will never know what differences alternative wordings make unless the different wordings have been carefully and systematically tested—a laborious process that many pollsters choose to avoid.

A general set of question wording problems has been identified by survey methodologists, and the problems that they represent for respondents have been studied extensively and are generally well understood. They include questions that use complicated language or have a complex structure; use a double negative; contain more than one question (double-barreled question); use leading phrases; or pose threats to respondents because they concern sensitive topics. Examples of each of these wording problems are discussed in detail below.

What is the problem of complex language in a poll question?

Many respondents cannot understand a poll question when it is phrased in terms of special language or it uses a complex structure. Poll questions have to be understood by every person interviewed, including those with the lowest levels of education and worldly experience.

Examples of poll questions that would be difficult for some respondents because of technical or complex language include:

> *Would you favor or oppose the government funding a Superconducting Super Collider?*

This is a high-energy physics device for learning about the fundamental nature of matter. Almost no one who is not a particle physicist knows very much about a superconducting super collider.

> *Do you think Congress should pass legislation to facilitate single-payer cost reimbursement plans for indigent patients?*

A respondent probably would have to be employed in some area of the health-care industry in order to have even a chance of understanding that this question refers to a proposed change in Medicaid. So the responses to such a poll question would not be very informative because they would be based on a faulty knowledge base or, in some cases, a guess about what the question means.

When pollsters are trying to measure opinions on important national issues whose details may be unfamiliar to many citizens, they sometimes use an introduction to the question to present background information on the issue. If these descriptions become too long or too complex in structure, respondents may lose track of the original intention of the question or important details of the issue they are being asked to express an opinion about. Here is an example of such a question wording:

> *The United States is negotiating a treaty with its neighbors, Canada and Mexico, called the North American Free Trade Agreement, or NAFTA. The purpose of the treaty is to reduce duties and tariffs on goods manufactured in one country and exported to the others. Do you favor or oppose passage of NAFTA in the U.S. Congress?*

The NAFTA treaty involved a number of complex issues, which is one reason that it took such a long time to negotiate, and the debate in Congress was extended as well. It was difficult for pollsters to frame simple, understandable questions to measure public opinion concerning NAFTA; it is sometimes hard to imagine what kinds of opinions could be measured with complex question wordings like this one.

What is a double negative in a question?

A question that involves a *double negative* poses a thought in such a confusing way that the pollster cannot be sure which form of the question the respondent is answering. As a simple example, suppose a pollster asked respondents whether they agree or disagree with the following statement:

> *Sometimes my life seems so uncomplicated that I cannot figure it out.*

The respondents have to figure out whether their lives are "complicated" or "uncomplicated" and whether or not they "can" or "cannot" figure them out, before they can decide whether they agree or disagree with the statement.

This may seem like an easy problem to avoid in wording questions, but one of the most interesting controversies in contemporary polling involved a question with an added negative in it. In 1993 the Roper Organization released data on Americans' beliefs about the Holocaust in which they suggested that almost one-quarter of Americans doubted that the Holocaust had occurred, much higher than equivalent proportions of from 1 to 5 percent of various European samples that were asked the same question.[9] This conclusion was drawn from responses to the following question asked of a representative national sample in the United States:

> *Does it seem possible or does it seem impossible to you that the Nazi extermination of the Jews never happened?*

In translating this question from the French, a pollster added another negative to the question and it clearly confused respondents and altered their answers. A series of question wording experiments subsequently conducted by the Roper Organization, the Gallup Organization, and CBS News clearly showed that the difference in U.S. response patterns could be linked to the double negative. When the same question was asked in the United States that was asked in the other countries, the distribution of responses was the same.

What is a double-barreled question?

As readers may recognize, wording poll questions so that they yield

9. See Tom W. Smith, "Poll Review: The Holocaust Denial Controversy," *Public Opinion Quarterly* 59 (Summer 1995):269–95.

unbiased and reliable data can be a considerable challenge for even the most skilled pollsters. But the mistake of writing a *double-barreled question* is a potential pitfall to which only a careless pollster is likely to fall victim.

A *double-barreled item* contains a question stem that poses more than one concept to the respondent, and that complexity is not clearly related to the alternatives offered in the response categories. Typically, a double-barreled question should actually be rephrased as *two separate items* because it really is asking respondents about two separate concepts. These concepts might be related, but in order to gather valid data, each must be asked about in a separate question.

Take the case of asking about a president's approval level with an item that combines two aspects of the president's job. As an example, think of the following question:

> *Do you approve or disapprove of the way the president is handling the country's foreign and domestic affairs?*

Answers to this item are almost meaningless for pollsters because they cannot know whether respondents who said "approve" really meant they approved the president's handling of *both* foreign and domestic affairs or approved of his handling of *only one* of these aspects of his job and disregarded the other in their answer. The same confusion would exist in trying to interpret the meaning of a *disapprove response*. That is to say, does "disapprove" mean disapproval of the president's handling of one or both types of policies? Consumers of poll results cannot interpret answers to double-barreled questions with any confidence.

Instead of linking two concepts in a double-barreled question, careful pollsters avoid the mistake by splitting the two concepts into two separate questions. Then the attitudes about each element of the president's handling of his job can be assessed independently and cleanly.

A general rule of thumb that readers can apply to evaluating poll questions for this problem is to look closely at items that contain the word "and." This is not to suggest that all items with "and" are double-barreled or that all double-barreled items contain "and." Nevertheless, many double-barreled items do contain "and"; thus it can be a useful tip-off in detecting them.

What is the effect of a leading phrase in a question?

A leading phrase in a poll question can frame the question in such a way that some respondents may be more inclined to agree or support a proposition that it contains or, in a different case, to disagree or oppose a proposition that it contains.

One typical example of how this works is a question that begins with a phrase indicating that the president supports the policy or that it is his policy. When questions are asked this way, especially in a period of an international crisis or conflict, experiments show that respondents are more likely to express support for the policy than if the question did not include that phrase. These differences would be found in the following two alternative forms of asking what is otherwise the same question:

> *Are you in favor of or opposed to sending American troops to assist in the NATO mission in Bosnia?*

as opposed to

> *In light of President Clinton's decision to send troops, are you in favor of or opposed to sending American troops to assist in the NATO mission in Bosnia?*

In another version of this framing issue, a leading phrase might indicate that many Americans support a particular side of an issue as a prelude to asking respondents for their opinions. Suggesting that many people hold a particular position can also produce more responses in support of that position:

> *Many Americans favor sending American troops to assist in the*

NATO mission in Bosnia. How about you? Do you favor or oppose sending American troops to assist in the NATO mission in Bosnia?

Are responses to questions on sensitive topics affected by how they are worded?

Responses to questions about sensitive topics can definitely be affected by how they are worded. Sometimes a single word or phrase can produce more responses in support of or in opposition to a public policy.

In many areas of controversial public policy, measurements of public opinion are highly susceptible to question wording. For example, a pollster who is measuring the electorate's attitudes toward the abortion issue will gather different attitudinal responses depending on whether or not the word "legal" is included in the item wording, as in the difference between the following questions:

> *Do you agree or disagree that a woman should be able to get a legal abortion for any reason of her choice in her first three months of pregnancy?*

and

> *Do you agree or disagree that a woman should be able to get an abortion for any reason of her choice in her first three months of pregnancy?*

Another important phrase in questions designed to measure opinions about government actions or proposed legislation involves the use of terms such as "forbid" and "allow." In general, Americans are much less likely to agree that the government should forbid certain forms of behavior than they should "not be allowed." Pairs of alternative questions posed in the following way will produce different patterns of response:[10]

10. This example can be found in Howard Schuman and Stanley Presser, *Questions and Answers in Attitude Surveys* (New York: Academic Press, 1981), 281.

> *Do you think the United States should forbid public speeches in favor of communism?*

as opposed to

> *Do you think the United States should allow public speeches in favor of communism?*

In response to the first question, 39 percent of a sample indicated "yes," such speeches should be forbidden. In the second case, 56 percent of a sample indicated "no," such speeches should not be allowed (should be forbidden).

Another factor affecting the public's response to public policy questions is the degree of specificity contained in the descriptions of the policies. For example, different questions asked in the fall of 1995 about U.S. involvement in Bosnia suggested different levels of support for President Clinton's actions. When ABC News posed the following question, 57 percent said they opposed the president's plan, while 39 percent supported it:

> *Clinton said now that a Bosnia peace treaty has been signed, he's sending 20,000 U.S. troops there as part of an international peacekeeping force. Do you support or oppose sending 20,000 U.S. troops to Bosnia as part of an international peacekeeping force?*

But the Gallup Organization, in a survey conducted for *USA Today* and CNN, found that 46 percent of the public supported the administration's plan and 40 percent expressed opposition when the question was asked in the following way:

> *Now that a peace agreement has been reached by all the groups currently fighting in Bosnia, the Clinton administration plans to contribute U.S. troops to an international peacekeeping force. Do you favor or oppose that?*

The use of the term "contributes" as well as the absence of the number of troops expected to go to Bosnia was cited as the explanation for higher levels of support in the Gallup survey than in the ABC News poll.[11]

Can the wording of a question be manipulated to produce a certain result?

The wording of a question can be purposely manipulated (*biased*) by an unscrupulous pollster in order to "push" respondents' choices in a direction the pollster desires. So consumers of polls have to evaluate descriptions of public opinion on an issue in terms of the exact questions that were asked.

Take the example of a pollster working for a candidate who advocates a certain environmental protection policy. The unethical pollster could strongly distort the proportion of the public who appear to support the candidate's policy if the question wording contained an unfounded or exaggerated listing of the damages that the environment might suffer if the policy were not put into effect, just as opinions could be affected by a phrase indicating that the policy could be "implemented without any significant increase in taxes."

Whenever possible, the careful consumer of poll results should always look at the wording of the items used in the poll. We believe that this is especially important for journalists, who too often use and disseminate poll findings without critically scrutinizing whether or not item wording might have biased the findings.

Do the response categories in a closed-end question make a difference in the responses that they elicit?

The words or phrases used for *response alternatives* can make as much difference in the pattern of answers that respondents provide as the wording of the question itself.

11. Richard Morin, "How Do People Really Feel about Bosnia? It Depends on How and When You Ask the Question," *Washington Post National Weekly Edition*, 4–10 December 1995.

It is important to recognize that the response alternatives offered for closed-end poll questions provide a *context* within which the pollster allows the respondent a choice. Although different polls might measure a concept with a *question stem* that uses exactly the same words—"How would you rate the president's performance on economic affairs? Would you say ... ?"—the items are technically different and may yield quite different data unless the available response alternatives offered to respondents are exactly the same.

For example, an item assessing an incumbent's job performance could use a variety of response alternatives, such as the following:

☐ "very good," "good," "fair," "poor," or "very poor"
☐ "good," "fair," or "poor"
☐ "A," "B," "C," "D," or "F"
☐ "acceptable" or "unacceptable"
☐ "satisfactory," "somewhat satisfactory," "somewhat unsatisfactory," or "not at all satisfactory"

Varied response alternatives provide different contexts, so they easily can lead to different answers. Unless items that measure the same concept with the same wording also use exactly the same response alternatives, then any observed differences in the pattern of answers between the items could merely reflect the different answer categories from which respondents picked. Does "good" mean the same thing when it is bounded by "very good," "fair," or "poor," as it does when it is grouped with "excellent," "fair," or "poor"? Its meaning is probably not exactly the same, but most likely it is quite close.

But what if "good" were used within the set of response alternatives "good, fair, or poor"? In this case, all respondents who thought the performance being rated was better than good are limited to "good" as their best choice. In contrast, the two earlier sets of responses provide the respondent a "better than good" category to choose, if that is the opinion the respondent holds.

So once again, let the poll consumer beware: comparisons

across poll items that purportedly measure the same concept, even when their *question stem* is worded the same, are very murky unless the wording used in the response alternatives of the items also is exactly the same.

What if a respondent is "undecided," "uncertain," or "doesn't have an opinion" on a question?

Another special problem with sets of response alternatives is whether or not they explicitly include a response for respondents who are uncertain of their opinions or likely behavior. Considerable past research has shown that having an interviewer read an explicit "don't know" or "uncertain" response choice—as in, "Do you agree, disagree, or are you uncertain?"—will elicit many more "uncertain" responses than if the interviewer does not explicitly offer such a choice. Thus, pollsters must constantly decide which approach they consider to be more valid: to add "uncertain" to the set of response choices that are offered explicitly to the respondent or not to do this.

Sometimes the "don't know" or "uncertain" option is not explicitly offered in the question wording itself, but the interviewer has instructions to accept such an answer and move on to the next question. This issue is further complicated by the different modes in which polls are conducted. In a self-administered exit-poll questionnaire, if "uncertain" is listed within the set of responses, the respondent will see it. In a telephone survey, however, an "uncertain" option is likely to be listed for the interviewer to mark *only if* respondents volunteer that they are uncertain.

What if a respondent gives a "don't know" response to a question?

Pollsters have done a considerable amount of thinking over the years about what to do with a respondent who says "don't know" (or its equivalent) when asked a poll item. They have considered two major yet separate issues: (1) How should an interviewer react to such a response? and (2) How should such a response be analyzed?

As a general rule of thumb, the problems caused by "don't know" responses can be markedly reduced if the wording of the poll makes respondents comfortable with admitting that they do not have an opinion about something that the poll is trying to measure.

In some cases, a respondent may simply be uncertain of which answer to choose. Here, it is not that the respondent does not have opinions about the issue but that the opinions are not fully formulated or the response alternatives the interviewer offered do not reflect the respondent's uncertainty. Take the example of a respondent who has both favorable and unfavorable opinions about a candidate. If these positive and negative opinions completely balance out each other in the respondent's mind, then this respondent will be hard put to pick an answer from "very favorable," "somewhat favorable," "somewhat unfavorable," or "very unfavorable." In this instance, many pollsters will establish a system by which their interviewers are trained to detect this uncertainty and treated it as an "undecided" response. The interviewer is given the discretion to record it as such.

In other cases, the pollster may have devised a series of follow-up questions that can be used to extract additional information from the respondent to determine whether or not the respondent is *truly* undecided or is leaning in one direction or the other on the issue. In election polls, a common form of the trial-heat question is:

> *If the election were held today, and Bill Clinton was the Democratic candidate for president and Bob Dole was the Republican candidate, which one would you vote for?*

Early in the campaign, relatively large proportions of respondents will indicate they are undecided, and the proportion may still be significant at the end of the campaign. These respondents who say they are undecided are usually asked a follow-up question of the form:

> *If you had to choose, would you say you were leaning toward Bill Clinton, the Democrat, or Bob Dole, the Republican?*

The presidential preferences can be tabulated with the "leaners" added in or left out, and the results can be reported in the same fashion as well.

In other instances, a respondent might be truly uninformed about an issue and not at all reticent about telling the interviewer, "I don't know anything about that!" In this case, the respondent's candor should be both valued and respected by the pollster because the validity of the data is improved by recording such candor. Unfortunately, *social desirability* forces many respondents to go ahead and give an answer from the choices the interviewer has provided rather than admit they do not have an opinion on or do not know about a public policy issue.

Some analysts choose to report data that exclude the "don't know" responses, effectively changing the sample size. Others include these responses as an indication of how informed the sample was about the issue under question. In the first case, the analyst should make clear that some respondents have been excluded from the analysis. The second case probably presents a more accurate representation of opinion on the issue.

Does the order in which questions are asked make a difference in the responses elicited?

Again, the answer is a definite yes! In addition to the words and the grammar used in a poll item, the placement of an item within the questionnaire can make a considerable difference in the answers that respondents give. Pollsters refer to this phenomenon as a *context effect* because the placement represents part of the *context* within which the measurement is taken.

The questions have to be asked in a certain order so that meaningful information can be collected. For example, there are two standard ways in which pollsters ascertain how familiar respondents are with the candidates. One concept is *recall,* and it measures the ability of the respondents to extract the names of the candidates from their memory. It is usually asked in the following form:

Do you remember the names of the candidates who are running for governor in this November's election?

A second concept is *recognition*. It is a less rigorous test of familiarity because it measures the ability of respondents to recognize the names of the candidates from a list they are given. It is usually asked in the following form:

I am going to read you a list of the names of candidates running for governor in this November's election. Please tell me if you recognize the name I read. If you do not, I will go on to the next name.

If a pollster is interested in both concepts, *recall* and *recognition,* then the unaided question (recall) has to be asked before the aided one (recognition) and not vice versa. There are other examples of the importance of structure, such as asking respondents to tell the interviewer what they know about an issue before beginning a series of questions that ascertain whether or not respondents agree or disagree with specific aspects of alternative policy proposals for dealing with the issue.

One classic example of order effects in election polls is associated with the set of items that ask the public to provide "approval ratings" of the incumbent president. Some polls simply measure overall approval of how well the president has been doing his job and always place this item at the very start of the poll. The Gallup Organization "invented" this question and has always placed it first in its questionnaires. Other polling organizations ask a series of questions about how well the president is doing on specific aspects of his job, such as in foreign and domestic affairs, in addition to an overall approval item. In the latter case, some pollsters place the overall approval item at the start of the sequence, before asking about specific aspects of the job. But some other pollsters place it at the end, after first asking about the specific job aspects. Past research on these context effects has consistently shown that asking the overall approval rating *before* the more specific ratings tends to elicit higher approval scores on the overall measure than when it is asked after a list of specific job approval items.

Order effects within questionnaires are one of the most well-documented "problems" with polls and surveys. Knowing this, many pollsters strive for accuracy by constantly testing their questionnaires for such effects. Unfortunately there is not always a practical solution to *eliminate* an order effect. Concerned pollsters who find themselves in such a predicament will randomly assign different question orders to different poll respondents and then see what difference order makes in the responses they get. For example, half a sample might be asked the overall approval rating *before* the specific ratings and the other half will be asked the overall rating *after* the specific ones. In this way, the pollster can measure any differences caused by the different item orders and then can try to adjust for the effects after the data are analyzed and before they are reported.

Are some questions typically asked early in an interview and others later?

Yes, there is a general pattern used to order the "sections" of items within most election poll questionnaires. Although there is some variation across the questionnaires used by different polling organizations, in many cases this is the basic pattern: (1) attitudes, (2) intentions and past behaviors, and (3) demographics and other background information.

There are two reasons that this general pattern is used. First, it makes for good "conversational rapport" between the interviewer and respondent. Second, this pattern is generally the one that is least likely to affect or distort the answers to subsequent questions.

Respondents become most readily engaged in a poll when they are asked interesting, nonthreatening, and not overly intrusive questions right at the start of the interview. In fact, sometimes pollsters will design an interview so that it begins with a question whose purpose is simply to help establish rapport. It has been found that asking people about their attitudes and opinions toward various political issues at the beginning of a questionnaire serves these purposes very well—such items are generally nonthreatening and are interesting (and easy) for respondents to answer. A common question used to begin a political poll is, "What do you think is the most important problem facing the country today?" This question has no "right" answer and indicates that the interviewer is interested in the respondent's assessments of current affairs.

After asking about opinions, it works well for the "conversation" to move on to items that measure a respondent's likelihood of voting and candidate preferences (*"If the election were held today, would you vote for . . ."*) and/or past voting behavior (*"In 1992, did you vote for George Bush, Bill Clinton, or Ross Perot?"*). Finally, the respondents are informed that the interview is wrapping up when they are told the interviewer has "just a few more questions about your background that can be used in analysis of your responses to the other questions." Many pollsters believe that the demographics fit better at the end because the respondents have been "warmed up" by the previous questioning and are more ready to provide personal information after knowing what else they were asked about. If a poll begins with demographic questions, respondents might feel threatened by personal questions about how much money their family earns, for example, without having any sense of what other information this response would be used to analyze.

The second main reason that pollsters use this pattern is that they think it has less potential for distortion (error) due to *question order effects*. Questions about opinions and attitudes are generally most sensitive to the context in which they are asked. Behavioral report items are less so, and demographic questions the least. Therefore, placing the opinion items first instills greater confidence in the validity of the responses they elicit than if they were placed after behavior items.

How do researchers know whether questions are biased?

Bias in a poll question refers to the *systematic error* that can be caused by its wording or its placement within a questionnaire. By systematic error, we mean inaccuracies that lead to a measurement that is higher or lower than what the "true" value is. For example, a bathroom scale that consistently overweighs people by five pounds is a biased measurement tool. The scale produces a faulty weight that is systematically off. Survey items can have the same kind of inaccuracy problem.

The best way to test for potential bias is to pretest questions. A *pretest* involves conducting a few interviews, not necessarily even from a probability sample of respondents, in order to see whether the questions are being understood, the response categories are appropriate, and information is being collected that corresponds to other known or reasonable distributions of opinion on the same issue. Some survey items are so blatantly biased that this is obvious once pointed out; in other cases, a pretest is required to demonstrate the problems that are present. Chapter 10 explains how unscrupulous pollsters may purposely introduce biased question wordings in order to influence poll results.

Nevertheless, there are many times when it is not at all obvious that a question may have a bias associated with it. Given the availability of resources (time and money), methodological checks can be incorporated into either a questionnaire or additional data analyses that can be performed after a poll is conducted—or both. Unfortunately, not many pollsters have the necessary resources or the interest to do this.

One of the best techniques to investigate possible question bias is the so-called *split-half* survey design. In this design, there is a *random assignment* of various question wordings or question orders to different subgroups in the sample.[12] Random assignment occurs whenever there are at least two versions of a poll item or ordering of items that need to be investigated; the randomization process is used to determine which respondents are asked which version. In the analysis, the response patterns to the two or more

12. The process of *random assignment* is used to manipulate the questions that are asked or the order in which they are asked. It should not be confused with *random sampling*, which is a process for selecting survey respondents so that they represent the target population.

versions of the questionnaire are compared to see if differences appear.

The split-half design is what other social scientists typically refer to as a *true experiment* to measure cause and effect relationships. If the analysis shows a significant difference that is associated with the different question wordings or orderings, then the pollster can confidently conclude that at least one of the wording or ordering versions is in some way "biasing" the data. But it often is not obvious what the pollster can or should do about this.

Are there other ways to test for bias in a questionnaire?

Another basic approach to detecting bias is to conduct additional data analysis to explore any patterns of correlations that would not be expected to occur if the questions were unbiased. This approach sometimes requires a difficult "judgment call" on the part of the pollster about whether or not a pattern of bias has been discovered. But, all things considered, it is better for pollsters to do such analyses and consider these issues than to ignore them.

For example, a pollster might find that answers to a particular question varied by the race of the respondent. This could be a signal that the wording or the topic of the question produced biased responses to the item. Sometimes this can occur for reasons such as *social desirability*, whereby respondents offer choices that they think the interviewer expects them to give.

Many elections in the United States involve contests between African American candidates and white candidates, and the number of these elections is increasing. Research in such contests in Virginia for governor and New York City for mayor has shown that polls conducted during such biracial campaigns result in white respondents overreporting their support for African American candidates.[13] They are even more likely to do this when they are inter-

13. For research on these issues, see Michael W. Traugott and Vincent Price, "Exit Polls in the 1989 Virginia Gubernatorial Race: Where Did They Go Wrong?" *Public Opinion Quarterly* 56 (Summer 1992): 245–53; Steven E. Finkel, Thomas M. Guterbock, and Marian J. Borg,

viewed by African American interviewers than by white interviewers. It is not always possible or feasible to match the race of the respondents and the interviewers in preelection polls in these campaigns. Knowing that these relationships exist, however, suggests that any data collected in such polls should be analyzed by race of respondent and race of interviewer to see whether differences in response patterns are observed.

In sum, there are many ways that researchers can try to learn if poll items are biased. Some are very straightforward, such as simply thinking logically about a blatantly atrocious item and correcting its deficiencies. In most cases, though, pollsters do not make obvious and colossal mistakes in writing biased questions. Instead, they must be willing and able to plan careful investigations of possible bias in their polls and to estimate the direction and magnitude of its effects.

References

BIEMER, PAUL P., ROBERT M. GROVES, LARS E. LYBERG, NANCY A. MATHIOWETZ, AND SEYMOUR SUDMAN, EDS. 1991. *Measurement Errors in Surveys.* New York: Wiley.
This advanced and technically sophisticated book contains chapters that review and document the state of scientific knowledge on measurement errors in surveys associated with the questionnaire, respondents, interviewers, and the survey mode. Attention is also given to the issue of "modeling measurement errors and their effects on estimation and data analysis."
The chapters on questionnaire design cover the order of items within questionnaires and the choice of response alternatives. Recent work on "cognitively designed" questionnaires is included. The sections on respondents and interviewers and the errors they can contribute to surveys include problems with recall, self versus proxy responses, interviewer training, and other topics. In addition to reviewing what is known about methods meant to reduce potential measurement errors, the book also covers techniques that can help estimate the nature and size of various

---

"Race of Interviewer Effects in a Preelection Poll," *Public Opinion Quarterly* 55 (Fall 1991):313–30.

measurement errors and shows some ways for using these techniques to make statistical adjustments to improve the accuracy of estimates.

BRADBURN, NORMAN M., SEYMOUR SUDMAN, AND ASSOCIATES. 1979. *Improving Interview Methods and Questionnaire Design.* San Francisco: Jossey-Bass.
This scholarly book uses the research findings from a joint research program on "response effects in surveys" that was carried out by NORC at the University of Chicago and the Survey Research Lab at the University of Illinois in the 1970s to describe and explain survey procedures that are likely to yield accurate reporting of answers by respondents. Readers need not be statistically sophisticated to be able to understand the text, but they will need a moderately advanced understanding of research methods for the book to be of value. The authors' intended audiences are survey data collectors and students and researchers of response effects.

The chapters deal with three causes of response effects: interviewer characteristics; respondent characteristics; and "variables that derive from the nature and the structure of the interviewing task." The effects of these factors are considered separately for attitudinal questions, nonthreatening behavioral questions, and threatening behavioral questions. For attitudinal questions, task variables were more strongly related to response effects than respondent-interviewer characteristics, except when the characteristics were related to what was being measured (e.g., racial attitudes). For both nonthreatening and threatening behavioral questions, respondent memory factors were most strongly related to response effects (more so in the case of the threatening questions), whereas interviewer-respondent characteristics were unrelated to effects.

CONVERSE, JEAN M., AND STANLEY PRESSER. 1986. *Survey Questions: Handcrafting the Standardized Questionnaire.* Newbury Park, Calif.: Sage.
This very brief volume (only 80 pages) in a series on quantitative applications in the social sciences is the standard introduction to designing and evaluating questionnaires. It consists of three chapters that the authors describe as "concentric circles" that move from the general to the specific and focus on the reader's particular research problem.

The first chapter is the most general, dealing with strategies for creating questions and highlighting a long list of cautions that a researcher should keep in mind. In the second chapter, the focus is on research findings about the impact of question wording and form. Much of this is drawn from the authors' own research. In the third chapter, the authors deal with evaluations of questions designed for a specific task—the importance of pretests, consulting with others, and listening to the comments of interviewers who conducted the pretest interviews.

ROBINSON, JOHN P., JERROLD G. RUSK, AND KENDRA B. HEAD. 1973. *Measures of Political Attitudes.* Ann Arbor: Center for Political Studies, ISR.

This "old" book from the Institute for Social Research (ISR) at the University of Michigan remains the single best compendium of questionnaire items and scales that measure a host of political attitudes. The book starts with a readable technical introduction to the scale-construction criteria the authors used in evaluating the ninety-five political attitudes scales they reviewed. For each topic area, the items in the measurement scales are listed, along with detailed information on the scale's reliability and validity.

The topic areas, each of which have a number of multi-item scales presented, include public reaction to government policies; liberalism-conservatism; democratic principles; domestic government policies; racial and ethnic attitudes; international affairs; hostility-related national attitudes; community-based political attitudes; political information; political participation; attitudes towards the political process; and a variety of individual political items, such as party identification, that are used in Michigan's election studies.

SCHUMAN, HOWARD, AND STANLEY PRESSER. 1981. *Questions and Answers in Attitude Surveys.* New York: Academic Press.

This book is the single greatest collection of experimental results that clearly demonstrate that survey responses are a function of what you ask and how you ask it. Schuman and Presser present the results of more than 200 question wording and order experiments that they conducted in multiple surveys.

Their work covers all the major topics in questionnaire design and its impact on survey responses. They include question wording and question order, open versus closed questions, assessment of "no opinion" by altering question form, measuring middle positions and issues of balance and imbalance in questions, and problems of response acquiescence. They also report results on intensity of opinions and attitude strength, and there is a very good chapter on tone of wording that includes discussions of the impact of question wording when asking about hot topics such as "abortion" (or "ending pregnancy" as an alternative).

SUDMAN, SEYMOUR, AND NORMAN M. BRADBURN. 1982. *Asking Questions*. San Francisco: Jossey-Bass.

In the authors' words, this is a "practical guide to questionnaire design," the type that would be used in social and market research. The structure and focus of this book builds on, and complements, the authors' earlier text, *Improving Interview Method and Questionnaire Design* (1979).

The book begins with a discussion of the social context of asking questions and introduces the authors' central thesis: "questions must be precisely worded if responses to a survey are to be accurate and the survey valid." The other chapters address nonthreatening behavior measures (e.g., routine, everyday behaviors, including shopping patterns), threatening behavior measures (e.g., exposure to drugs, alcohol, various sexual experiences, and the like), knowledge questions meant to determine how much a respondent knows about a topic, and attitude questions.

An entire chapter addresses the issue of response alternatives in closed-end questions. Another chapter focuses on the ordering of items within a questionnaire, and two other chapters deal with structural and format issues in laying out a questionnaire. The final chapter explains the overall process that is used to develop a questionnaire and stresses the importance of pilot testing and multiple revisions before a questionnaire is actually ready to use in real data collection.

The book, like others of its vintage, is somewhat dated, as it was written at a time when new advances in the application of cognitive psychology to questionnaire design had not yet been made.

8

How Do Media Organizations
Analyze Polls?

Media organizations have to analyze and present the results of polls in a way that is understandable and intelligible for readers and viewers with limited methodological and statistical training. Usually, this means that poll data are analyzed and presented one variable at a time. Sometimes there is limited analysis of the data by the demographic characteristics of the respondents, such as age, race, or sex. Often, however, there is no analysis by relevant subgroups. Then the audience member is left with a statement of gross percentages or rates that are technically "accurate" but do not provide any politically useful or relevant basis for interpretation.

A general problem with many media polls is that a good deal of time and money is invested in collecting the data, but too little effort is devoted to analysis. This situation tends to be worse for data presented on television than for data in a print format. Television stories are shorter and require that some of the content be devoted to graphics. Some critics of the analysis of media polls describe them as "data rich but analysis poor," reflecting the fact that better stories could often be told with the data available, if more skillful analyses were presented.[14]

14. This phrase is used by Richard Morin of the *Washington Post,* as quoted in Lavrakas, Traugott, and Miller, *Presidential Polls and the News Media,* 12.

How is a poll analyzed?

Each question in a poll is converted to one or more variables that can be analyzed by statistical software. In modern polling, where most of the data are collected through telephone interviews, the questionnaires themselves are computerized. As the interviewer records a respondent's answers, they go directly into the computer. This means that in these computer assisted telephone interviewing (CATI) applications, the data are available for analysis as soon as the last interview is completed.

The use of CATI applications also means that the results can be analyzed and reviewed at various stages during the interviewing period, such as at the end of each day. This is important to news organizations because these interim analyses help reporters to think about and structure their stories in advance and to discuss this coverage with their editors or producers. Of course, the preparation of the final story must wait until all the data are in; but interim analyses are an important part of the newsmaking process.

What is a variable?

A *variable* is a measure that contains the range of responses to a question. By definition, a variable consists of different categories associated with different responses, as opposed to a *constant,* in which all of the responses are the same.

In a simple case, there may be information recorded about respondent characteristics, such as gender or age. Every respondent to a survey is either "male" or "female," so gender is a variable with two categories. The respondent's age can be recorded in several ways. One would be to record actual years of age. In a survey of teenagers, where the age range is constrained, this might be useful for analysis. But in a general population survey of adults, this would require too many categories and could complicate analysis because of the sheer number of responses. So in these cases it is common to bracket ages into groupings like "18 to 24 years of age," "25 to 45 years of age," "46 to 64 years of age," and "65 years of age or older." In these instances (gender and age), the categories are inclusive of all the possible responses, and each is mutually exclusive. That is, each response can fall into one and only one category.

What are the frequencies?

Frequencies consist of the raw numbers of cases (interviews or respondents) coded with each value of the variable. The raw numbers are not usually as important analytically as their "relative" occurrence, which is most easily presented and interpreted as percentages or proportions.

That is, it is not important to know that 356 respondents "approve" of the way Bill Clinton is handling his job as president because the significance of that number depends on how many people were interviewed. It is more useful to know that 53 percent of the respondents "approve" of Bill Clinton's handling of his job as president, 36 percent "disapprove," and the remaining 11 percent are "undecided" or "don't know" how they feel about him.

Therefore, most news articles report poll data as percentages. Good reporting will provide the percentages for each category of the variable, except when there are only two variables and the assumption can be made that the second percentage is 100 percent minus the first.

What is an estimate?

An *estimate* is a statistic calculated from a sample used to conduct a poll, and it represents a statistical statement of what the "true" value is likely to be in the population, if everyone were to be interviewed. A preelection poll can be used to estimate the turnout in next week's election, for example. Or a survey might estimate the unemployment rate in the population during the past month.

Assuming a probability method of sampling was used, the precision of these estimates is based on the size of the sample from which the information was collected, as described in chapter 5. A sample estimate has some error associated with it (the margin of error) due to chance alone. This translates into a level of confidence that the estimate accurately reflects the "true" or population value of the statistic.

A poll might produce an estimate of turnout in the election that is stated as "52 percent, with a margin of error of plus or minus 3 percentage points and a 95 percent confidence level." The translation of this is that 52 percent of the survey respondents indicated that they are likely to vote. Probability theory suggests that 95 out of 100 samples of the same size would produce an estimate of turnout between 49 and 55 percent.

What is a relationship between two variables?

The essence of analysis is comparison; and one variable, sometimes called an *independent variable,* can be used to predict or explain why some subgroups in the sample are different from each other on a second variable, called a *dependent variable.* Using appropriate explanatory (independent) variables makes analysis of poll data politically relevant and interesting.

For example, the "gender gap" is a concept that suggests that men and women evaluate candidates differently and frequently support them to different degrees. In order to analyze the gender gap, pollsters look at the candidate preference question by gender to see whether or not the proportion of women who prefer candidate A is greater or less than the proportion of men who prefer candidate A. If there is a difference, then the gender gap is present; if there is no difference, then the gender gap is absent. This principle of analysis is illustrated in tables 8.1 and 8.2.

TABLE 8.1

CANDIDATE PREFERENCE

BY GENDER

	Prefer A	Prefer B	Total
Men	58%	42%	100%
Women	55%	45%	100%
Total	56%	44%	100%

TABLE 8.2

CANDIDATE PREFERENCE

BY GENDER

	Prefer A	Prefer B	Total
Men	64%	36%	100%
Women	48%	52%	100%
Total	56%	44%	100%

In both surveys, candidate A is preferred over candidate B by a 56 to 44 percent margin. In table 8.1, there is no real difference (at least one that is statistically significant) in the proportion of men and women who prefer candidate A; since men and women are about equally represented in the electorate, there is no difference in the support for candidate A that appears in the population as a whole. In table 8.2, however, candidate A is the clear choice of men, while women are equally divided in their preferences. The "gap" in preference for candidate A by gender is 16 percentage points. The second survey produces content that is inherently more interesting and newsworthy because the analysis shows a different pattern of support by subgroup than the first survey.

How do the media typically present poll results?

The typical poll story in the media is organized around the main "finding" from the survey and sometimes is embellished with information from standard reportorial techniques such as interviews with candidates or their campaign managers. If there is time or space available, additional data may be presented from other questions that were part of the survey. The most common form of data presentation includes the marginal frequencies for the main question and perhaps some breakdowns of those data by demographic groups, including party identification.

Often a news organization is interested in adding a human dimension to the sterile presentation of numerical data. So reporters may interview people and add photographs or video to the story. In some cases, they interview people who were part of the sample, after these respondents waive their right to confidentiality. In other instances, reporters just go out to get useful quotes by interviewing as many people as are necessary. The "representative" attitudes are obtained from the poll by employing scientific sampling techniques. Knowing what the poll results are, a reporter can then search out interesting and appropriate prototypes of the respondents who can provide good quotations or sound bites.

There are some differences in the way results from the same

poll will be presented on television and in a newspaper or magazine. Most televised presentations of poll data involve only a single story because space is much more scarce in the newshole of a twenty-two minute evening news broadcast (a half hour minus the commercials) than it is in a newspaper. The televised version of the story usually will include tabular presentation of data, but print stories often do not contain data tables. Newspapers often will print a "methods box" containing some of the details of how the study was conducted. Television stories usually provide only the sample size and an indication of the size of sampling error.

Is the presentation of marginals misleading?

The presentation of *marginal frequencies* can be misleading if it gives the impression, often false, that public opinion is solidified or that views are strongly held. Providing marginals without any breakdown by relevant subgroups may also produce a less interesting story than one that has the nuance of appropriate analysis.

As an example, questions were raised early in the 1992 primaries about Bill Clinton's fidelity after a woman held a press conference and claimed she had had an affair with him. In response to the press conference, many news organizations sponsored or conducted polls asking questions about the public's view of a candidate who had been unfaithful to his wife. Most of these polls showed that a majority of Americans felt such a person would not make a good candidate, and many journalists concluded that the Clinton candidacy was in trouble.

Subsequent analysis of these data suggested that those who were most concerned about the fidelity issue were Republicans and others who had already decided to support George Bush. People who had decided to support Clinton were less concerned. It also turned out that people who were registered to vote were less concerned than unregistered citizens. When analyzed in this fashion, the poll suggested that the Clinton candidacy was probably *not in trouble*, especially since the allegations were not proven.

What is a trend?

A *trend* reflects the analysis of the responses to a single question administered repeatedly over different surveys. That is, if a series of polls contains questions on presidential approval, the trend in the data can be analyzed to see whether approval is increasing, decreasing, or staying about the same.

A very common form of trend analysis in election polls involves looking for changes in the "trial heat" question, the question that measures the relative standing of the candidates. A political campaign is all about swaying public opinion to put together a winning coalition on Election Day. Furthermore, this form of analysis is consistent with the media's preoccupation with "horserace journalism" (who is ahead and who is behind) and the use of sporting metaphors to characterize the strategy and performance of the competitors.

How are trends analyzed?

There are actually two ways that polls are used to analyze trends. One is through the administration of the *same question to different samples* at different points in time, and the other is through the administration of the *same question to the same sample* at more than one point in time.

The first case employs a design involving what is known as *repeated cross-sections,* whereby the same question is asked in successive polls, each involving its own sample. You can have the greatest confidence in trend analysis when the amount of change is relatively large (greater than sampling error), and the time series of polls involves more than two measurements. Looking at trends over time is complicated with only two data points because they always result in a "straight line" projection that must suggest movement upward, downward, or at a constant level. If the longer-term movement is much more complicated than that, measurements from only two polls will not adequately reflect that complexity.

In order to estimate the full amount of change, pollsters must employ a *panel design* in at least two studies. In a panel, the same people are interviewed at more than one point in time and are asked the same question. The full extent of change at the individual level can be measured in this fashion.

How can surveys measure change?

Understanding the different ways that repeated cross-sections and panel designs measure change is an important tool in interpreting poll results, especially as they apply to politics.

For example, the president's approval rating may be 44 percent one month and 54 percent the next. If the two independent polls have sufficiently large sample sizes so that the margin of error is, say, plus or minus 3 percentage points, then we are reasonably confident in concluding that the president's approval rating has risen because the range from 41 to 47 percent does not overlap with the range from 51 to 57 percent.

But this change of 10 percentage points is an aggregate measure, reflecting the net difference between people who felt more positively about the president across thirty days and those who felt less positive about him. By interviewing the same people in both months and comparing their answers from each survey, four groups of respondents can be identified: (1) those who approved of the president in both months, (2) those who disapproved of the president in both months, (3) those who approved at first and then disapproved, and (4) those who disapproved at first and then approved. The size of the latter two groups is greater than the 10 percentage-point difference, although their combination is where the difference came from. These groups can be analyzed thoroughly only when the same people are interviewed at more than one point in time.

What does it mean that public opinion has "changed"?

This is a more complicated issue to deal with because one form of "change" refers to different proportions of the public holding attitudes on an issue. That is essentially what is involved in the trend analysis discussed above.

Another form of change refers to the public holding different attitudes. And the notion of "holding different attitudes" can be a direct result of the use of different questions in different surveys. This is one of the most difficult matters of interpretation of multiple polls on the same issue. To make direct and accurate comparisons of change, the same questions must be asked of similar individuals with the results coded in the same fashion.

Is it possible to compare data collected in different polls?

The answer is, it depends. And the factors that make the answer conditional are the question asked, the people who were asked the question, and the significance of the time that elapsed between the two surveys.

One way to think about these issues is through the following example. You read a newspaper article that contains the statement that "polls show that President Clinton's popularity has declined in the last three months." This is a statement about change that appears to be based on polls. The central concept here is "President Clinton's popularity," which is typically measured in a single survey question. The minimum condition for comparing the president's popularity would be that the same question was asked in more than one survey, that is, that the question had the same wording and included the same response categories. If two different questions were asked, it is sometimes impossible to evaluate the meaning of the responses, even if the response patterns were apparently the same. So you would want to know the exact question wordings. The importance of this is discussed in greater detail in chapter 7.

A second issue is who was asked the question. If the responses in the early survey were obtained from a representative sample of all Americans and those in the later survey were obtained from a representative sample of Republicans, we would not be surprised to know that Republicans have less favorable views of President Clinton than a sample that contained many Democrats and Independents.

Finally, we would want to know whether any significant events occurred in the period between the first and the second surveys. This might explain why attitudes toward President Clinton had changed between the first and second surveys, suggesting that the change in fact was in an expected direction.

What does it mean when poll data are weighted?

Weighting refers to certain statistical adjustments that often are made to the "raw" data that the sampled respondents provide. These adjustments take place before the data are analyzed, in an attempt to improve the accuracy with which the data for the sampled respondents, such as their voting intentions and opinions, reflect those of the target population.

Weighting is generally done for two purposes. Whenever a probability sample is used and the respondents have had an *unequal* chance of being sampled, weighting can be used to balance the probabilities of selection so they reflect an "equal chance of selection" for each respondent. In telephone polls, this is done by adjusting for the number of telephone lines in the household and for the number of voting-age residents in the household. So, for example, each person who has two telephone lines might receive a weight of "1/2" to compensate for the fact that he or she was twice as likely to be selected as someone with only one line.

A second purpose of weighting is to try to "correct" for the nonresponse that is present in every election poll. For example, women are typically easier to reach in polls that last only a few days than are men, and thus most polls will interview proportionately more women than their actual percentage of the population. Whereas women make up about 54 percent of the adult population in the United States, it is not unusual for an election poll to end up with a sample that is 60 percent or more female. If women, as a group, are more likely to vote for a certain candidate than are men, then unweighted poll data that reflect an oversample of women will misrepresent the target population's actual voting intention for that candidate. In this example, women might receive a weight of "54/60" before the pollster began to analyze the data. Problems of nonresponse are discussed in detail in chapter 5.

A difficulty with weighting to adjust for nonresponse is that the pollster cannot be certain that it will have the intended consequence of improving the survey's accuracy. This is another area where the "art" of polling, as opposed to the "science," comes into play in the use of election poll data.

Reference

WEISBERG, HERBERT F., AND BRUCE D. BOWEN. 1977. *An Introduction to Survey Research and Data Analysis.* San Francisco: W.H. Freeman.
This little book is divided into two parts: an introduction to survey design that takes up the first third, and an introduction to data analysis that occupies the rest of the text.
The first part of the text covers the standard issues of sampling, questionnaire design, and interviewing. It also includes a useful chapter on coding. It is difficult to find an equivalent treatment of data analysis that is as concise and nontechnical as this one. The coverage includes univariate frequencies and bivariate distributions, measures of association, and the preparation of research reports.

9

How Can I Evaluate Published Poll Results?

Many citizens are inherently skeptical about polls and poll results. As a poll consumer, you want to have confidence in the information you see or read. There are only a few simple things you need to know in order to make an informed judgment about the quality of the data and the findings based on them.

Some people are concerned about "small" sample sizes: How can I trust information obtained from so few people? Why should I believe poll results if no one I know has ever been interviewed?

Some people are concerned about the presentation of biased data by individuals or groups who want to use polls to support views they already hold: How do I know they asked the "right" question? Which group of people responded to this poll?

Still others are uncomfortable with statistical information because it is unintelligible to them: What do all these numbers mean?

A few simple principles and rules will help any citizen to understand and evaluate poll results—if the report of the poll contains the appropriate information. The preceding chapters introduced the essential elements of this information. Some readers may have skipped ahead to this chapter in order to find a short list of items they should consider in evaluating poll results. This chapter contains a summary of information that will help readers perform a critical review of published poll results.

What do I need to know to understand and interpret poll results?

In order to interpret the published results of a poll, a reader or viewer should know who sponsored the poll, who conducted the poll, and a certain level of detail about how the poll was conducted. The latter information includes specific details about the questions asked, who the respondents were and how they were sampled, and the dates when the poll was conducted. With this information in hand, poll consumers can make up their own minds about what the data mean and how much faith they want to put in the results.

Are there any standards for reporting poll results?

Fortunately, the polling industry and those who work in it have been very concerned about standards for reporting survey results. Two national groups of professionals have developed such standards. The American Association for Public Opinion Research (AAPOR) is an organization whose members are individuals who produce and use survey data; they have a Code of Professional Ethics and Practices. The National Council of Public Polls (NCPP) is an association of organizations that conduct polls. They have a set of Principles of Disclosure to guide the publication of poll results. Copies of both sets of standards are included in the appendix.

The AAPOR and NCPP standards are very similar, although they do differ in some significant ways. There is a long list of items that both organizations agree should be disclosed in reports, press releases, or other public dissemination of poll results. They include the sponsorship of the survey and who conducted it; field dates for the interviewing; the method of obtaining the interviews; the population sampled and the size of the sample and any subsamples; the complete wording of questions asked; and base for the percentages on which the conclusions were based. The AAPOR standards further suggest including information about sampling error or precision and any information about weighting procedures. They also suggest including information about completion rates, eligibility criteria, and screening procedures.

When the results from a poll are published in the newspaper, this information is usually placed in a "methods box" found at or near the end of the article. When the results are used in a television broadcast, much less information of this kind is usually made available. Often, the viewer will only see the sample size and the margin of error estimate.

Why do I want to know who sponsored the poll?

This is a poll consumer's first, best guide to whether the results might be biased in some fashion. When polls are sponsored by a candidate, for example, they might have been intended for strategic use in the campaign. So question wordings might be unusual in some way. Sometimes poll results are leaked to reporters on a "confidential" or "exclusive" basis that is clearly intended to get them published or broadcast. Under those circumstances, a reader should wonder whether the most favorable results were released while others were withheld.

Sometimes a special-interest group interested in influencing proposed legislation will sponsor a poll. Recently, a series of similar polls was sponsored by the Citizens Flag Alliance, a group that is supporting a constitutional amendment to prevent burning of the American flag. Separate surveys were conducted in ten states whose U.S. senators had indicated they were undecided about this issue. These polls were conducted and released to the public in an attempt to influence future votes in the Senate and citizens who might vote in the senators' reelection campaigns.

Why do I want to know who conducted the poll?

Polls are conducted by well-known national polling firms, as well as by other, less skilled companies. Most people cannot evaluate polling firms unless additional information is provided about their history or some of their recent clients. But poll consumers who know the name and location of the firm can use this information to contact the company to request additional information about the poll.

If the poll results were released at a press conference, then both the AAPOR and NCPP standards suggest that the polling organization should answer poll consumers' questions about the methodology of the poll or the results.

Why do I want to know what kinds of interviews were conducted?

Information about what kinds of interviews were taken can tell a poll consumer something about other important considerations, such as the likely response rate. Telephone interviews usually produce higher response rates than mail surveys, which typically have very low response rates. Telephone interviews are usually conducted over a very short period, while mail surveys take much longer. A relatively short interviewing period is important for media polls because events may have taken place between the time the first and last interviews were obtained, influencing the interpretation of the results.

A poll consumer also wants to know whether information was obtained from people who volunteered their responses by calling an "800" or a "900" number to register their views or by clipping a questionnaire from a newspaper or a magazine. These "call-in" or "mail-in" polls of self-selected respondents present substantial concerns of bias. These issues are discussed in detail in chapters 6 and 10.

Why do I want to know what kind of sample was used?

The most important issue is whether the poll used a probability design or not. If not, then inferences from the sampled opinions to those of the population cannot be made reliably. The laws of probability and inferential statistics can be used only when every member of the population had a known, nonzero probability of selection. If that is not true, it is likely that biases were present in the sampling procedures.

Information about the sampling frame is important too. Telephone directories are not good frames for telephone interviews, for example, because reliance on this source for numbers will exclude those who have unlisted numbers or have moved recently. These issues are discussed in chapter 5.

Why do I want to know what the sample size was?

Knowing the sample size for a probability sample will tell a poll consumer something about the margin of sampling error around estimates produced from the poll. The larger the sample, the smaller the sampling error. A table of standard sampling errors is included in the appendix. But there are just a couple of numbers that a poll consumer might remember and use as a rule of thumb in evaluating poll data.

A useful guide is that the margin of error around an estimate for a sample of size 2,000 is ±2 percentage points. For a sample of size 1,000, it is ±3 percentage points; for a sample of size 500, about 4.5 percentage points; and for a sample of size 250, about 6 percentage points.

Why do I want to know if the responses of important subgroups were analyzed separately?

The estimates of sampling error given above are based on analysis of all the data. The analysis of subgroups in the sample is the same thing as producing estimates from samples of that reduced size, so the sampling errors are larger.

In most surveys of the general population, for example, the sample will contain about as many men as women. An estimate of President Clinton's approval rating in the full sample of size 1,000 will have a sampling error of ±3 percentage points. For the subsamples of men or women, however, the margin of error for an equivalent statistic will be ±4.5 percentage points. Although the sample is half the size, the margin of error is only about 50 percent greater.

Why do I want to know what the response rate was?

The response rate is one indication of how well the sample design was carried out. When the response rate gets unacceptably low, usually below 75 percent of the original sample, you should be concerned about whether the sample adequately represents the population from which it was drawn, even if a probability method was used.

In particular, a low response rate may suggest a problem of bias in the selection of respondents. Were the people who refused to participate in the survey different in some substantively relevant way from those who did participate? Is this really a survey of people who are "interested in politics" because those who refused to be interviewed were not interested? Or was the field period so short that many people were away from home or otherwise unavailable? Are the people who could not be reached different in any substantive way from the people who could be reached? These issues are discussed in chapter 5.

Why do I want to know when the interviews were conducted?

There are two issues here. Poll consumers want to know whether the data being reported are current and whether any important intervening events occurred while the poll was being conducted or since it was conducted.

Poll consumers generally assume that data contained in a poll report are current, especially if the newspaper or television station sponsored the poll because of its assumed news value. One important criterion of newsworthiness is that the story relates to something that is of current interest or that happened recently.

On occasion, a poll story contains data collected some time ago, such as information from candidate polls conducted at the start of the campaign. Candidates may release such data because the poll was favorable to positions they hold or to them personally. But a lot may have happened in the campaign since the data were originally collected, making it reasonable to assume that the same question asked last week would have produced a different result.

It is also important to know when data were collected in order to assess whether any intervening events occurred that might have affected public opinion. If the president makes a major policy address to the American people, a news organization wants to assess public opinion after the speech. Or if a crisis occurs in foreign affairs, a news organization wants to know about public opinion following those events. Sometimes, journalists are interested in whether opinions have changed because of the speech or the crisis. Then they want to compare data that were collected before the event with other data collected after it.

Why do I want to know the exact question wordings, including the response categories?

Knowing the exact question wording provides an indication of whether the question could be understood by the respondents, and it allows an evaluation of potential bias. If the question was closed-end, the wording will show what response alternatives were offered. The full wording will also show whether an explicit "don't know" category was included as an option. All of this information is useful for interpreting the meaning of the reported results.

Why do I want to know the question order?

Sometimes questions can be posed in a leading fashion, that is, in a sequence that is likely to produce a certain response to the last question in a series. Responses to a particular question should be evaluated, in part, by what questions came before it. It is often interesting to know what questions followed, to get an indication of whether the first set of responses might have affected some subsequent ones.

Why do I want to know whether there are references to other polls on the same topic?

If a published report of poll results contains a reference to other polls on the same subject, then it probably also contains statements about how opinions have changed over time. Provided with enough relevant information of the kind we have been discussing, a poll consumer can evaluate the previous results. This is the basis for assessing whether attitudes, opinions, or behaviors have really "changed."

Does the analysis suggest that changes in opinion have occurred and are such interpretations justified?

The meaning of change is a difference in "comparables." Sometimes, a discussion of change over time really reflects differences in measurement over time (completely different results) rather than change in the same measurement. To make direct and accurate assessments of change requires a comparison of the responses to the same question, asked of similar individuals, and with the results coded in the same fashion.

Poll consumers should look to see that the same question was asked of respondents in two similar samples, if not of the same respondents interviewed at more than one point in time. The same question wording means that the same concept, such as presidential approval, was measured. If the same polling organization conducted both surveys, it is more likely that this is the case.

It is also important to note whether the same kinds of people were asked the question. Often the findings from two polls will be reported as presenting conflicting results. In the first poll, the question was asked of a representative sample of the entire population; but in the later one, it was asked only of partisans of one kind or another (Democrats or Republicans). Another common problem is that results from the trial-heat question appear to change because it was asked of a sample of "adults" or "registered voters" in an early poll, but it was asked of "likely voters" as Election Day neared.

References

ASHER, HERB. 1995. *Polling and the Public: What Every Citizen Should Know.* 3d ed. Washington D.C.: CQ Press.
Asher's easy-to-read book provides a good overview of the place of polls—not just election polls and surveys—in American society. His goal is to help citizens become wiser consumers of the information gathered

via polls. As a political scientist, he is especially concerned about the problem of "nonattitudes"—the troubling tendency of respondents to give answers to questions about which they have no thoughtful opinions—and explains how serious pollsters can try to counter the damage this problem can do to poll results.

The book provides a mostly nontechnical explanation of the main segments of polling methods, including questionnaire design (the wording and ordering of questions), sampling techniques, and interviewing methods and the possibility of interviewer-related error. Asher explains how the news media use polls and the problems inherent in many news reports based on polls. The book also includes one chapter on election polls that touches on many of the most important issues, such as how to deal with undecided voters and how to estimate voter turnout. The book concludes with sections explaining and illustrating how poll data are analyzed and interpreted and concludes with a useful "miniguide" to help readers "evaluate" poll quality.

Bradburn, Norman M., and Seymour Sudman. 1988. *Polls and Surveys: Understanding What They Tell Us.* San Francisco: Jossey-Bass.
This nontechnical book is aimed at "newcomers to public opinion measurement," and various postsecondary-level students of public opinion and market research. While somewhat similar in purpose to the present volume, the structure is different. Bradburn and Sudman have provided "answers to the questions frequently asked by respondents in surveys, by those who have not yet been selected as participants, and by journalists, businessmen, and many others who have to deal with survey data." It shares the mission of the present volume, and several other of the books reviewed here, in trying to educate consumers of polls.

The book begins with a review of the purposes of polls and of general survey methods, including a historical review of the growth of public opinion polling. Chapters focus on "proper and improper" uses of survey research and whether or not polls should be legally restricted. The effects of polls on society are also discussed. Other chapters address issues of sampling, data collection and analysis, questionnaire wording, and sources of survey error. A chapter unique to this book is the one that describes the diversity that exists across survey organizations, from those in academe to those in the private sector.

Gallup, George H., 1948. *A Guide to Public Opinion Polls.* Princeton: Princeton University Press.
In many ways, this volume is the forefather of the current text. It used a

question-and-answer format and was produced with nontechnical language for a popular audience. For Gallup, this volume was also a way to promote the new method that he was working with and make its details more accessible to the general public. The reader will find it entertaining to compare the treatment of the same topics in this book to Gallup's work of almost fifty years ago.

Sections deal with topics that are continuing themes in election polls—sampling, questionnaire design, and interviewing, for example. But there are also sections that deal with the function and role of public opinion polls in democracy. There is a great deal of concern with prediction and accuracy as well.

Almost half a century of intervening research has of course changed the answers to some of the questions, just as polling methods have changed in that period. For example, a current treatment of sampling would no longer contain an extended description of the value of quota sampling.

GALLUP, GEORGE H. 1972. *The Sophisticated Poll Watcher's Guide.* Princeton: Princeton Opinion Press.
This volume is dedicated to the daily newspapers of America that had the foresight to make public opinion data available to the masses, through Gallup's weekly columns and those of his contemporaries. This volume is only broadly organized around questions that serve as focal points for Gallup's commentary on public opinion and its role in democracy, the importance of polls as measures of public opinion, and election polls and the prediction of elections.

The text is organized into three sections, representing the themes of questions that Gallup was frequently asked by readers and political elites with whom he discussed public opinion procedures and findings. The first section contains a discussion of the purposes that polls serve in a democratic society. The second section contains a discussion of the methodology of conducting polls. The final section contains commentary on election polls in particular, including forecasting and accuracy. The appendix contains a very interesting chronology of the highlights in polling history.

LAKE, CELINDA C. 1987. *Public Opinion Polling.* Washington, D.C.: Island Press.
This is an interesting volume because it suggests ways that public interest groups can conduct their own polls. While this is a problematic approach that is fraught with the danger of collecting poor-quality data, the book is

nevertheless valuable for the lists of problems it contains and the suggestions for dealing with them, including checklists of points to remember.

While the book is composed of ten chapters, it can be thought of as organized into four parts. The first three chapters provide the introduction, explaining what polling is and looking at the relative merits of face-to-face, mail, and telephone polls. There is a chapter on questionnaire wording and construction, followed by two chapters on interviewing. An extensive chapter on sampling covers many of the practical issues of designing, drawing, and managing a sample. Two chapters describe data processing and analysis. The final chapter contains a review that emphasizes possible sources of error and ways of dealing with them.

10

WHAT ARE SOME COMMON PROBLEMS AND COMPLAINTS ABOUT POLLS?

With all of the knowledge about polls and the polling process that you have gained by getting this far into the book, it is possible now to talk more about the promises and the pitfalls of polling.

On the positive side, the prospects for election polls contributing to a better-informed citizenry are virtually unlimited. In order for that potential to be realized, however, polls have to be conducted with care so that they produce reliable and valid data. They have to be analyzed carefully so that accurate and meaningful news stories are constructed from them. And these stories have to be produced and disseminated in ways that reasonably large numbers of sophisticated readers and viewers will be exposed to them. The main purpose of this book has been to provide readers with the background knowledge to become educated consumers of polling information.

The pitfalls are numerous too. Many news organizations, especially individual television and radio stations and smaller newspapers, are enamored of polls as a news source. Editors and producers want to generate their own data at the lowest cost possible. In the polling business, just as in any other, you get what you pay for. One difference, however, is that you can disseminate an awful lot of bad data very quickly through the application of modern technology to the news business.

Many journalists attach a special weight to information obtained from press releases and press conferences that an individual or a special-interest group has called to discuss some new poll findings. When poll results are "redisseminated" through news organizations in this manner, it is the responsibility of journalists to serve as gatekeepers for data quality. This will require additional training in basic polling methods and the elements of data analysis for most of them. And contrary to the standards for determining newsworthiness that places an emphasis on what has happened in the past twenty-four or forty-eight hours, journalists must learn that sometimes they will have to return to a poll-based story from some time ago to reexamine reports of public opinion at that time.

For example, at the end of 1995, a controversy arose over statements made in 1994 about public support for the "Contract with America." Information of some kind, perhaps from a combination of focus groups and a survey, was collected and disseminated to suggest that "at least six out of ten" Americans supported every plank of the contract. Revisiting and reconstructing events at that time, Frank Greve, a reporter for Knight-Ridder, has concluded that these statements, which formed the basis for a story in the *Wall Street Journal* and subsequently appeared in innumerable news stories and the *Congressional Record*, were misleading at best and possibly false. There was no representative sampling of adult Americans who were asked balanced and unbiased questions about the policy preferences on these matters. This lack of "true" public support is one factor among many that appears to explain why the Republicans in Congress have had such difficulty in converting the contract into legislation, and the party in general and some of its leaders in particular have suffered in subsequent measures of public opinion as a result.

These kinds of issues, and many others like them, are dealt with in the answers to the following questions.

Do polls measure "real" attitudes?

One of the main reasons for election polls is to measure the electorate's thoughts on a wide variety of social policy issues, such as balancing the federal budget, abortion, capital punishment, and welfare reform. Pollsters often refer to the ideas that the public holds about these policy issues—an aggregated kind of "public opinion"—as the public's *attitudes*.

A common concern that poll critics (and many pollsters themselves) have about *measures of attitudes* taken in polls is whether or not they represent anything "real" beyond the context of the poll. There is wide variation in any population in terms of how interested people are in public policy issues and how much thought they have given to specific policy proposals. Experience with polls has demonstrated convincingly that many adults answer an opinion question in a poll, such as, "Do you agree or disagree that the United States should send emergency aid to Haiti?" *without* having given much thought to the specific issue prior to being asked the question. Under these circumstances, some critics argue that the "attitudes" measured by the poll do not reflect "public opinion."

One form of *measurement error* is produced by respondents who answer a question inaccurately. There are many reasons why this might happen, including not wanting to appear uninformed or ignorant. Therefore, some respondents choose one of the answers (such as "strongly disagree") offered in the poll question rather than admit they are uninformed about an issue by saying "I don't know."

The issue of whether or not the attitudes that pollsters measure are real has been the subject of much research and debate—too much to review here. Nevertheless, pollsters have one fairly easy-to-implement solution to help cope with the problem of respondents expressing attitudes on issues they know little or nothing about. They can add questions to polls to "test" the accuracy of respondents' knowledge about an issue and then they can conduct subsequent analysis by dividing respondents who are relatively "informed" or "uninformed" into subgroups. The purpose of this is to investigate differences in the opinions and policy preferences they hold. Such a comparison does not directly answer the question of whether the attitudes are "real," but it does go a long way in providing a broader understanding of attitudes that are expressed. Unfortunately, this straightforward approach is often judged "impractical" by pollsters (and their sponsors or clients) because it lengthens interviews, thereby adding to costs.

There are also many times when "knowledge" is irrelevant to the poll's purpose. Candidates often sponsor private polls to learn what the public thinks about an issue, not necessarily whether citizens know much about it or not. The reason these private polls treat these attitudes as real is that they can affect the way that citizens will vote, regardless of whether or not they are well informed on an issue. Even uninformed attitudes can have very real consequences for candidates!

Can polls be designed to find whatever the sponsor wants?

As explained in chapter 7, there are many ways that a questionnaire can be formulated that can lead to "biased" findings. Sometimes these flaws are intentional because they are explicitly planned by the pollster (and possibly the sponsor) to lead to a knowingly biased but nonetheless desired result. This practice is abhorrent to any ethical pollster, but that does not mean that the practice does not take place. In fact, professional organizations such as the American Association for Public Opinion Research, the American Marketing Association, and the National Council of Public Polls work to root out such practices and censure those who engage in these unethical practices. Their enforcement procedures are often limited, but their efforts at exposing such practices are important for maintaining public confidence in the polling business.

An example will help illustrate how poll questions can purposely be written to lead to "desired" findings. Imagine an unscrupulous pollster who wanted to publicize poll results unfavorable to an opposing political candidate. The pollster would merely need to word certain attitude questions in such a way that candidate X's policy positions appeared to be at odds with some revered figure in American politics, even if that person never really held such a position. By explicitly linking a policy position with a respected public figure, the pollster would lead many respondents to be more likely to side with that position and against candidate X's position, even if they actually were generally supportive of the same side of the issue as candidate X. The unscrupulous pollster would then typically hold a press conference or issue a press release to report the opposition to candidate X's position, without an explicit reference to the leading question that was asked. In this way, the pollster would have manipulated and biased the measures in order to create a certain result, and the misleading result would be entered into the news stream by further deceit.

When is a "survey" not a survey?

Another unscrupulous practice in which some "pollsters" and telemarketers engage is to pretend that a legitimate survey is being conducted when in fact it is not a survey at all! This flagrant violation of business ethics is different from the problem of purposely biasing the wording of poll questions in order to shape the answers that are likely to be given. In these instances, we are talking about "pollsters" pretending to conduct a survey when something else entirely is really occurring.

One such unethical practice is a form of the infamous *push polls*. This type of push poll mimics a legitimate survey, but its real purpose is to manipulate public opinion for strategic purposes. This is accomplished by pretending that the respondent has been contacted for a legitimate poll and then using purposely biased questions that are laden with propaganda supportive of the candidate or the issue position the pollster is trying to "push" public sentiment toward. Unsophisticated respondents in a push poll may never realize that they were *not* interviewed for a poll in which there was sincere interest in their opinions; instead, they were interviewed because the pollster wanted to expose the respondents to propaganda masquerading as survey questions.

When telemarketers engage in a similar practice, it often is referred to "SUGing," or *soliciting under the guise* of polling. In these cases, telemarketing sales personnel pretend to be legitimate telephone interviewers calling to conduct a survey. But they are really using the simulated survey to establish enough interviewer-respondent rapport to give the respondent a sales pitch. Telemarketers who engage in this unscrupulous practice have found that many more people will stay on a telephone line long enough to hear the sales pitch if they start out thinking they have been called for a survey than if the sales pitch is made explicit right from the start of the conversation.

The same principle applies when a pseudo poll is used to raise money for a special-interest group. A series of unbalanced questions are asked that lead many of the respondents to conclude that the special-interest group needs financial assistance. This practice is known as "FRUGing," or *fund raising under the guise* of survey research.

What is an audience call-in poll?

For the past decade or so, more and more radio and television stations have started to conduct *call-in polls* of their listeners and viewers. The basic approach is to pose a single question designed to elicit opinions from the audience and to provide telephone numbers for the audience to call. Usually two numbers are offered, each associated with a different answer to the poll question, such as "agree" and "disagree." This method also is occasionally used by daily newspapers; in these cases, the newspaper typically prints two telephone numbers associated with an equivalent two-choice decision, such as agreement or disagreement with an issue.

Typically, these numbers are provided so that callers can register support either for or against an issue, but the method also can be used to register preferences for different candidates contesting an election. Sometimes the telephone numbers are local ones for which the caller does not pay anything. Other call-in polls use free "800" numbers for the audience to call to register their opinions, if long-distance charges would otherwise deter callers. Still other call-in polls, some of which border on questionable ethics, use "900" numbers, which cost the caller a fee, often less than $1 but sometimes a lot more. These polls are used for fund-raising purposes by whoever is conducting the poll. Such a technique was used by Ross Perot in his 1992 presidential campaign.

Audience call-in polls suffer terribly from major sources of survey error. In particular, there is absolutely no control over who is "sampled," since callers are self-selected and may call in as many times as they choose without the pollster knowing this has happened. Furthermore, the questions posed usually offer too restrictive response alternatives, typically only two options from which to choose. Although a count might be taken of the number of "agree" or "disagree" calls, these polls typically ignore any measurement of the undecided sentiment, which can sometimes be of considerable size. As a result, the responses are typically biased by calls from people who have strongly held views on the issue.

One interesting application of the call-in poll in 1992 illustrates the problems the practice presents.[15] After President Bush's State of the Union address on 28 January, CBS News sponsored a call-in poll to get viewer reactions. For some measures, they had results from a scientifically conducted poll from just a few days earlier. All told, they tallied about 315,000 responses out of 24.5 million calls attempted. Among the call-in poll respondents, 29 percent said they were "better off" than they had been four years ago, 53 percent said they were "worse off," and 18 percent said they were "the same." From the regular CBS poll conducted 14–19 January that used a probability sample, the responses were 24 percent who said they were "better off," 32 percent who said "worse off," and 44 percent who said "the same." So the people who dialed and made it through to have their opinions registered were much more concerned about their personal financial circumstances than was the public as a whole.

Call-in polls might be considered legitimate vehicles for building audience interest in a radio or television program or among a newspaper's readership, but they have no scientific value whatsoever for anyone who wants to sample voters' opinions or

15. "What Was Wrong with the CBS News 800 Number Call-In Poll?" *Public Perspective*, March/April 1992, 18–24.

preferences with any accuracy. This is not to say that the results of call-in polls are always wrong; however, the people who conduct these polls have no way of knowing whether they are right or wrong. This circumstance is itself basically the same as always being wrong.

With the application of new computer-based technology, some media organizations, especially local television stations, are using automatic dialing machines with digitized voices of their anchors to conduct "polls" in just a few hours. These *computerized response audience polls,* or CRAP as they have been called, can produce 1,000 "interviews" in just a few hours by continuous dialing. They obviously involve sampling with replacement, and there is no designated respondent because they accept the responses of anyone who answers the phone. They can be used to produce "factoids" for the 11 P.M. news, based on breaking events of the day. Even though they may involve large numbers of interviews, they are unscientific polls because of inadequate sampling and respondent selection.

How should I treat polls that are mailed to my home?

Receiving a questionnaire in the mail provides the recipients with the opportunity to exercise the option of whether or not to respond without the pressure they might feel if the contact was made by an interviewer via telephone or by knocking on the front door. The decision to participate in a poll should always be viewed (and presented) as a voluntary act—one that will bring no harm to potential respondents, regardless of whether they agree to participate or not.

In deciding whether to take the time to respond to a mail survey, you should consider the same basic factors that would affect your decision to participate in any survey. The most important of these are as follows:

1. Is there an explanation of who is conducting and sponsoring the study?

2. Is there an explanation of the purpose of the study?

3. Is there an assurance that your answers will be kept confidential?

4. Is there an explanation of who is being sampled and how the sample was chosen?

5. Is there a telephone number that you can call if you have any questions or want to check on the legitimacy of the study?

6. Does the questionnaire appear to have been crafted in an unbiased fashion, with questions that are easy to understand and response choices that logically fit the questions being asked?

For any of the above questions, a "no" answer is a strike against the pollster. When reviewing this list in the context of a particular request to be interviewed, citizens will ultimately need to make their own decisions depending on how the poll "scores" on this list. We suggest that if even a few of these questions are not addressed in the covering letter or instructions you receive with the mail poll, you should err on the cautious side and not respond. We say this with confidence because almost all well-conceptualized and legitimate polls will more than adequately meet these standards.

Some additional considerations you can use to make a final decision about whether or not to respond to a mail poll include whether or not a stamped self-return envelope was provided. A "no" is a strike against the pollster. Was company letterhead used on the correspondence? Again, a "no" should make you wonder about the professionalism and legitimacy of the pollster. Finally, does the poll follow up with a postcard or some other second (or third) mailing to encourage you to respond as soon as possible? Once again, a "no" suggests a poll that is not striving for accuracy. Any poll that does only one mailing, without follow-up contacts, is likely to have a dismally low response rate and is unlikely to produce valid and reliable data. Why would you want to participate in a poll that is not likely to be accurate?

How accurate are insert polls that you find in magazines or newspapers?

Newspapers and magazines are constantly striving to build reader loyalty, and one way they have found to do this is to provide readers with opportunities to participate in the "news" process. Encouraging readers to write letters to the editor has been the traditional mode for this. With the explosion of access to the Internet, readers nowadays are often given the e-mail addresses of editors so they can more quickly and easily express their opinions.

Yet another technique to create audience involvement is to let readers fill out a survey questionnaire that is printed in the newspaper or magazine. Low response rates undermine the accuracy of many mail polls, especially those inserted into newspapers and magazines. Even when many of these insert polls now provide readers with the opportunity to fax in the questionnaire (which is almost always a single page in length), this does not appreciably increase the proportion of readers who respond. Thus, the people conducting insert polls have no way of knowing whether or not the responses they receive are representative of their target population.

As with call-in polls, those conducting an insert poll will neither have a good idea of who has selected themselves into the "sample" nor how many times any one person has done so. Sometimes basic demographic questions are printed on insert polls, but these demographics cannot be used with any confidence to determine whether or not the "sample" accurately reflects the opinions and preferences of the target population (whatever that is). This information can only be used to show whether the demographics of the sample match the larger readership, if it is the newspaper's or magazine's readership that is defined as the target population. There is no way to calculate the margin of error for such nonprobability samples, further eliminating any clue as to the likely accuracy of the results.

Polls inserted into newspapers and magazines are vehicles for engaging readers and building reader interest in, and loyalty to, the publication. They are not a method that can be used to measure people's opinions and preferences in any reliable fashion.

If I receive a telephone call to be interviewed, should I participate?

The reader might be surprised to learn that many people who are interviewed for well-conceived and well-executed polls enjoy the experience. The reason for this is that professional interviewers who work for a high-quality polling organization tend to enjoy their work, and this is reflected in the manner in which they interact with respondents. They respect and value respondents' rights to express their opinions honestly, and they sincerely convey their appreciation when a respondent participates.

As explained in the answer to the question about mail surveys, there is a variety of "legitimizing" information that a high-quality telephone poll should provide to a potential respondent. Even if the interviewer's introductory statement does not explicitly contain the types of information enumerated in the discussion of that question (pp. 152–53), the interviewer should be trained (and authorized and instructed) to provide such information to every respondent who requests it. Any time an interviewer cannot or will not provide reasonable answers to reasonable queries posed by a respondent, respondents have good cause to wonder whether or not their time should be spent responding to the poll. High-quality telephone polls will be conducted from a centralized telephone center with a supervisor on duty to oversee the work of interviewers. A curious respondent should always be able to speak to the supervisor if desired. Interviewers who state that they do not have a supervisor should be considered suspect, either because they may not work for a high-quality polling organization or because the caller may not really be an interviewer.

Many potential respondents to telephone polls are concerned about how their telephone number was chosen, especially if they have an unlisted telephone number. The interviewer should be able to explain the process of random-digit dialing—as discussed in chapter 5—to the potential respondent's satisfaction. Otherwise, the respondent has good cause to choose not to participate.

Ultimately, respondents should be certain that their answers to survey questions will be kept confidential and that no harm will come to them from participating in a telephone poll. If respondents do not have this level of confidence, then they should not answer questions posed by the interviewer "stranger."

Suppose I am called at a bad time, like when I am sitting down to dinner?

High-quality telephone polls will try hard to complete interviews with everyone who falls in their sample. They are interested in achieving a high response rate, thereby lessening the chance for nonresponse error. One way this is done is by making callbacks to reach people when they are available and at a time that is convenient for them. So if you are eating dinner or otherwise engaged, and it is not convenient for you to be interviewed at that time, feel free to explain the poor timing of the call. An interviewer should simply respond by apologizing for the inconvenience and asking when a good time would be to call back. Any other response is simply not good interviewing practice, and you should be suspicious.

How do I know if a poll is being conducted by a reputable survey organization?

If you have never heard of the survey organization that is conducting the poll, then you may feel the need to confirm that the group is legitimate. A simple way to do this is to ask the interviewer for additional information about the organization, such as where they are located, and for a telephone number that you can call to verify that information. Many polling organizations now maintain "800" numbers that are toll free, just for this purpose. Even if you think you know or recognize the group doing the poll, you may still want to verify its legitimacy (and existence) before proceeding with the interview.

Ultimately, you will have to rely on your common sense to decide whether or not the group is legitimate and whether you should participate in the survey.

What can I do if I am contacted by a "pseudo poll"?

There are several professional associations of surveying and polling organizations that try to root out poor-quality and unethical polling practices. Some of the most prominent of these groups are the American Association for Public Opinion Research (AAPOR), the National Council of Public Polls (NCPP), and the Council of American Survey Research Organizations (CASRO). Each of these organizations welcomes questions from the public about survey practices and comments on questionable polling practices, such as pseudo polls. Contact information for two of these organizations is contained in appendix A.

What assurances should an interviewer give that nothing bad will happen to me if I participate in a poll?

Interviewers who work for high-quality polling organizations should be thoroughly trained to explain to respondents that their cooperation is entirely voluntary. They should also explain that their responses will remain totally confidential and that the poll data will be reported only in aggregated statistical form. These pledges mean that your answers will not be seen by anyone other than the interviewer and the people at the polling organization who process the data for computer analysis. Furthermore, employees of the polling organization should have signed their employer's "confidentiality statement," in which they pledge to never violate the confidentiality of the information that respondents provide.

On rare occasions a polling organization may want to deviate from these common ethical practices, but the legitimate poll will always seek and receive the explicit approval of the respondent in these cases. One exception is a media-sponsored poll where the news organization may be interested in having a reporter call back a poll respondent for an in-depth interview to gather quotes to use along with some of the respondent's answers to the poll questions as reported in a news story. The interviewer should ask whether or not you would be willing to speak to a reporter, and the reporter should always get your explicit permission to interview you and your agreement that the conversation will be "on the record."

References

CRESPI, IRVING. 1989. *Public Opinion, Polls, and Democracy.* Boulder, Colo.: Westview Press.
This short volume contains a concise review of the potentials for and problems with polls, linking technical and philosophical issues. Its strength is the discussion of the relationship between public opinion and policy and the intermediary role of polls in the process. It presents issues of polling methodology in a cogent fashion that requires no statistical background on the part of the reader.

The last two chapters on the relationship between news, polls, and democracy summarize all the main issues that are continually under review and dispute. Crespi is concerned about the possibility that the expanded use of polls by news organizations will undermine democracy, rather than strengthen it. He sees this as a function of two problems they have to overcome. One is the nature of the topics covered in polls, and the other is a reporting style that makes the results inaccessible to most members of the audience. Both problems must be solved in order for media polls to fulfill their potential.

FALLOWS, JAMES. 1996. *Breaking the News.* New York: Pantheon Books.
This book summarizes the current arguments raging in the journalism world about the "appropriate" role of news organizations in informing their audience. It discusses a litany of problems, how they arose, and the ways in which news organizations are addressing them.

It pays particular attention to the "public journalism" movement as a source of the solution. An important element of this debate is the role of public opinion and support among citizens and the degree to which news organizations should promote discussions of important issues rather than simply report the "news." In this regard, polls have become an important focus, especially the degree to which they should be used to inform news organizations of the issues that interest their readers and viewers, guiding subsequent coverage.

YANKELOVICH, DANIEL. 1991. *Coming to Public Judgment: Making Democracy Work in a Complex World.* Syracuse: Syracuse University Press.
Yankelovich, a social critic and pollster, presents a bleak assessment of the effects the news media have on America's search for public policy solutions to the nation's and the world's problems. He believes that a crucial concept "missing" from American democracy is a set of terms to describe the quality of public opinion and to distinguish good public opinion from bad.

Yankelovich provides a somewhat lengthy yet compelling treatise on how the news media and others should learn to distinguish between good-quality public opinion and bad. He details the barriers formed by devising public policies that rely too heavily on the "judgment of experts" and relying too little on the "wisdom" of the public. Nevertheless, he makes it clear that this wisdom—he calls it "public judgment" to distinguish it from "mass opinion"—does not exist on all policy issues. Yankelovich challenges the news media to help develop this wisdom in the citizenry. As defined by Yankelovich, public judgment exists on an issue when the citizenry's measured views are stable, consistent, "and most important of all, ... those who hold the opinions recognize the implications and take responsibility for them."

EPILOGUE

As we noted at the beginning of this book, election polls play a powerful role in contemporary American democracy. They can and do affect the candidates and their campaigns; reporters, editors, and the campaign coverage that their news organizations provide; and the attitudes, candidate preferences, and voting behavior of the public.

We believe that election polls used to their best and fullest potential could have a significant positive impact on the American electorate, in part because of their singular ability to provide an accurate reflection of the attitudes and preferences of the people on a timely basis.

Too often, their potential for good is not realized, whereas their potential for harming democracy seems to manifest itself routinely. Candidates and campaign strategists appear to use polling more often to determine merely how to beat an opponent rather than how best to serve the public. Journalists and their news organizations appear to use polling more often than not to help identify likely winners, whom they then decide will "merit" news coverage, rather than to identify, investigate, and portray the appropriate complexities of issues that can and should affect public policy formulation. Given the typical content and format of reporting based on media polls, the electorate appears to use polling results too often to decide whether or not to vote rather than to further educate themselves about their own domestic and foreign policy opinions and inform themselves before making their final candidate choices.

We believe that an educated public must demand better from its political activists, its news organizations, and itself. One of the ways this can happen is for more citizens to develop a better under-standing of the strengths and weaknesses of election polls, in part so they can make better use of this information in forming their own political judgments.

Appendix A

Standards
for Disclosing Information
about the Methodology
of Public Polls

*The American Association for Public Opinion Research (AAPOR)**

Code of Professional Ethics and Practices

We, the members of the American Association for Public Opinion Research, subscribe to the principles expressed in the following code. Our goals are to support sound and ethical practice in the conduct of public opinion research and in the use of such research for policy and decision making in the public and private sectors, as well as to improve public understanding of opinion research methods and the proper use of opinion research results.

We pledge ourselves to maintain high standards of scientific competence and integrity in conducting, analyzing, and reporting our work in our relations with survey respondents, with our clients, with those who eventually use the research for decision-making purposes, and with the general public. We further pledge ourselves to reject all tasks or assignments that would require activities inconsistent with the principles of this code.

*Office of the Secretariat, Box 1248, Ann Arbor, Michigan, 48106. Telephone: 313-764-1555; fax: 313-764-3341.

THE CODE

I. *Principles of Professional Practice in the Conduct of Our Work*

    A. We shall exercise due care in developing research designs and survey instruments, and in collecting, processing, and analyzing data, taking all reasonable steps to assure the reliability and validity of results.

        1. We shall recommend and employ only those tools and methods of analysis which, in our professional judgment, are well suited to the research problem at hand.

        2. We shall not select research tools and methods of analysis because of their capacity to yield misleading conclusions.

        3. We shall not knowingly make interpretations of research results, nor shall we tacitly permit interpretations that are inconsistent with the data available.

        4. We shall not knowingly imply that interpretations should be accorded greater confidence than the data actually warrant.

    B. We shall describe our methods and findings accurately and in appropriate detail in all research reports, adhering to the standards for minimal disclosure specified in Section III.

    C. If any of our work becomes the subject of a formal investigation of an alleged violation of this Code, undertaken with the approval of the AAPOR Executive Council, we shall provide additional information on the survey in such detail that a fellow survey practitioner would be able to conduct a professional evaluation of the survey.

II. *Principles of Professional Responsibility in Our Dealings with People*

    A. The Public:
        1. If we become aware of the appearance in public of serious

distortions of our research, we shall publicly disclose what is required to correct these distortions, including, as appropriate, a statement to the public media, legislative body, regulatory agency, or other appropriate group, in or before which the distorted findings were presented.

B. Clients or Sponsors:
  1. When undertaking work for a private client, we shall hold confidential all proprietary information obtained about the client and about the conduct and findings of the research undertaken for the client, except when the dissemination of the information is expressly authorized by the client, or when disclosure becomes necessary under terms of Section I-C or II-A of this Code.
  2. We shall be mindful of the limitations of our techniques and capabilities and shall accept only those research assignments which we can reasonably expect to accomplish within these limitations.

C. The Profession:
  1. We recognize our responsibility to contribute to the science of public opinion research and to disseminate as freely as possible the ideas and findings which emerge from our research.
  2. We shall not cite our membership in the Association as evidence of professional competence, since the Association does not so certify any persons or organizations.

D. The Respondent:
  1. We shall strive to avoid the use of practices or methods that may harm, humiliate, or seriously mislead survey respondents.
  2. Unless the respondent waives confidentiality for specified uses, we shall hold as privileged and confidential all information that might identify a respondent with his or her responses. We shall also not disclose or use the names of

respondents for non-research purposes unless the respondents grant us permission to do so.

III. *Standard for Minimal Disclosure*

Good professional practice imposes the obligation upon all public opinion researchers to include, in any report of research results, or to make available when that report is released, certain essential information about how the research was conducted. At a minimum, the following items should be disclosed:

1. Who sponsored the survey, and who conducted it.
2. The exact wording of questions asked, including the text of any preceding instruction or explanation to the interviewer or respondents that might reasonably be expected to affect the response.
3. A definition of the population under study, and a description of the sampling frame used to identify this population.
4. A description of the sample selection procedure, giving a clear indication of the method by which the respondents were selected by the researcher, or whether the respondents were entirely self-selected.
5. Size of samples and, if applicable, completion rates and information on eligibility criteria and screening procedures.
6. A discussion of the precision of the findings, including, if appropriate, estimates of sampling error, and a description of any weighting or estimating procedures used.
7. Which results are based on parts of the sample, rather than on the total sample.
8. Method, location, and dates of data collection.

March 1986

The National Council on Public Polls (NCPP)*

PRINCIPLES OF DISCLOSURE

We, the member organizations of the National Council on Public Polls, hereby affirm our commitment to standards of disclosure designed to insure that consumers of survey results that enter the public domain have an adequate basis for judging the reliability and validity of the results reported.

It shall not be the purpose of this Code to pass judgment on the merits of methods employed in specific surveys. Rather, it shall be our sole purpose to insure that pertinent information is disclosed concerning methods that were used so that consumers of surveys may assess studies for themselves.

Any survey organization, upon providing evidence to the Council of its compliance with this Code, shall be permitted to state that it "complies with the Principles of Disclosure of the National Council on Public Polls."

To the above ends, we agree with the following Principles of Disclosure and procedures to be followed in the event question is raised about compliance with them.

PRINCIPLES

All reports of survey findings of member organizations, prepared specifically for public release, will include reference to the following:

- □ Sponsorship of the survey;
- □ Dates of interviewing;
- □ Method of obtaining the interviews (in-person, telephone, or mail);
- □ Population that was sampled;
- □ Size of the sample;

---

*Suite 300, 1375 Kings Highway East, Fairfield, Connecticut, 06430-5318. Telephone: 800-239-0909; fax: 203-331-1750.

□ Size and description of the subsample, if the survey report relies primarily on less than the total sample;

□ Complete wording or questions upon which the release is based; and

□ The percentages upon which conclusions are based.

When survey results are released to any medium by a survey organization, the above items will be included in the release and a copy of the release will be filed with the Council within two weeks.

Survey organizations reporting results will endeavor to have print and broadcast media include the above items in their news stories and make a report containing these items available to the public upon request.

Organizations conducting privately commissioned surveys should make clear to their clients that the client has the right to maintain the confidentiality of survey findings. However, in the event the results of a privately commissioned poll are made public by the survey organization, it shall be assumed that they have entered the public domain and the above eight items should be disclosed.

In the event the results of a privately commissioned poll are made public by the client and the client acknowledges the release, the survey organization (a) shall make the information outlined above available to the public upon request and (b) shall have the responsibility to release the information above and other pertinent information necessary to put the client's release into the proper context if such a release has misrepresented the survey's findings.

Appendix B

Sample Tolerances (Sampling Errors) for Samples of Different Sizes

The data in the following table can be used, under an assumption of simple random sampling, to calculate the confidence interval around estimates based on samples of different sizes. It is based on a sample that is evenly divided in two halves on a measure, that is, 50 percent each. This produces the maximum confidence interval. The confidence interval would be smaller for proportions that are more extreme or divided, say 80 percent to 20 percent, in an equivalent sample of the same size. These calculations also assume that the samples are drawn from a population of at least 10,000.

For example, a survey based on a simple random sample of 1,500 respondents reports that 52 percent support Bill Clinton and 48 percent support Robert Dole. Using this table, you could conclude that 95 percent of the time, the proportion of people in the population who support Clinton lies between 49.5 percent and 54.5 percent (52 percent ± 2.5 percent).

It is important to remember that analysis of subsamples implies that a different row of the table must be referenced for the appropriate confidence interval. For example, the typical sample of adults in the United States would include about half male and half female respondents. So a sample of 1,500 respondents would consist of approximately 750 males and 750 females. While the confidence around an estimate of Clinton support in the entire sample should be ±2.5 percentage points, for the subsample of either men or women, it would be ±3.6 percentage points.

On some occasions, published polls report differences in the proportion of the sample that supports each candidate. In this case, the sampling error for this difference in proportions is about twice the sampling error for the estimate of each individual candidate's support.

TABLE B.I

CONFIDENCE INTERVALS

Sample size	Confidence interval at the 95% level (in percentage points)	Confidence interval at the 99% level (in percentage points)
50	13.9	18.8
100	9.8	12.9
250	6.2	8.2
500	4.4	5.8
750	3.6	4.7
1,000	3.1	4.1
1,250	2.8	3.7
1,500	2.5	3.3
2,000	2.2	2.9
2,500	2.0	2.6
5,000	1.4	1.8

GLOSSARY

AAPOR The American Association for Public Opinion Research. A professional organization whose members are engaged in the study of public opinion. This includes individual private-sector, academic, and government survey researchers. AAPOR was founded in 1946 to promote high-quality survey research and to encourage public disclosure of the methods and purposes of polls and surveys. (*See also* NCPP; CASRO.)

Advance contact An attempt to alert or "warm up" sampled respondents to the fact that they have been chosen to participate in a poll. This is typically done by sending a letter notifying them that they soon will be contacted by an interviewer. The advance contact usually explains the nature and purpose of the study, who is sponsoring it, who is conducting it, and what assurances of confidentiality the respondents can expect. (*See also* Cover letter.)

Approval ratings Closed-end poll questions used to measure the extent to which the public approves of the manner in which the president (or some other elected official) is handling current domestic and foreign policy issues facing the nation. The questions employ responses that often range from "strongly approve" to "strongly disapprove." These measures have been taken several times each year for half a century and often are used to contrast approval levels of a current elected official with previous holders of the same office. (*See also* Favorability ratings.)

Attitudinal questions Closed-end poll questions to measure enduring or general "beliefs" about various political issues. Often posed as statements to which a respondent is asked to "agree" or "disagree." For example, "A woman should be able to get a legal abortion for any reason of her choice. Do you strongly agree, agree, disagree, or strongly disagree?"

Balanced question A closed-end poll question with a question stem that poses both sides of an issue (e.g., "Some people favor an amendment that would require the federal government to have a balanced budget, whereas other people oppose such an amendment ...") and/or one that uses a range of responses that have a true midpoint (e.g., "very good, good, fair, poor, or very poor").

Bandwagon effect A "going with the winner" effect that causes some voters, who otherwise would be expected to vote for one candidate, to support another candidate who the preelection polls predict will win the election. Definitive research on this effect is very difficult to conduct and therefore not much is known with relative certainty about the effect. (*See also* Underdog effect.)

Bias Systematic error in poll data that consistently produces findings that differ from the "true" results or the value that exists in the entire target population. This can be caused by any of a number of factors, such as poor question wording, poor interviewing, low response rates, or poor sampling designs. Poll bias is like a bathroom scale that consistently overweighs everyone who steps on it by ten pounds. In some cases, unscrupulous pollsters can devise methods that purposely bias findings in desired directions.

Biased question A poll question whose wording consistently causes respondents to answer in a way that distorts their "true" opinions or preferences, thus leading to inaccurate measurements of the topic of interest. For example, the question wording, "Do you favor or oppose a woman's right legally to kill her fetus by having an abortion?" would cause fewer people to say "favor" than would be the case with less extreme (biased) wording.

Bivariate frequencies A statistical presentation of data that compares answers to two questions simultaneously. In election polls this is typically done by comparing responses to an opinion or preference question (the dependent variable) by the responses to a demographic question (the independent variable). For example, a report of poll results might contain a comparison of the proportion who say they approve or disapprove of the president's policies by the age of the respondents (those who are 18–29 years old, 30–44 years old, 45–59 years old, and 60 years or older).

Callbacks In face-to-face household polls and in telephone polls, the attempts made by interviewers to reach respondents who were not contacted in previous stops at the household or in previous dialings. Callbacks lessen survey nonresponse and may therefore lower nonresponse error. Media polls typically can manage few callbacks because news deadlines force the polls to be conducted over just a few days' time, sometimes even less.

Call-in polls Unscientific polls, most often sponsored by the news or entertainment media, which publicize telephone numbers that a self-selected respondent can call to register an opinion on a specified topic. Some use "800" or "900" numbers, while others simply use local phone numbers. Their value as accurate measures of public opinion is nil, but they do serve an "audience engagement" purpose. (*See also* 800 poll; 900 poll.)

Candidate preference An expression of a respondent's (likely) vote choice, at least as of the time the poll is conducted. Some undecided respondents are asked follow-up questions to determine toward which candidate they are "leaning." (*See also* Trial-heat question.)

Candidate recall The ability of respondents to remember the name of a political candidate on their own, in response to the question, "Can you tell me the names of the candidates who are running for (an office)?" (*See also* Candidate recognition.)

Candidate recognition The ability of a respondent to recognize a candidate's name when it is presented. This is the lowest level of a respondent's "knowledge" about a candidate. Awareness of the candidate's name is a necessary condition for having opinions about the candidate. Respondents are more likely to have difficulty in recognizing candidate names early in the campaign or at the time of primaries, as well as those of candidates running for down-ballot offices compared to such offices as president, governor, or U.S. senator. (*See also* Candidate recall.)

CAPI Computer assisted personal interviewing. Face-to-face surveys in which the interviewer uses a computer to proceed through the questionnaire and simultaneously enters the answers into a database that is quickly available for analysis. CAPI's advantages are the great control it affords over elements of the design of the questionnaire, such as randomized ordering of certain items and the accurate entry of data in an easy-to-analyze format.

CASRO Council of American Survey Research Organizations. An umbrella organization of professional groups and firms that engage in polling and other forms of survey research. CASRO's objectives are to maintain high standards of quality across the survey research industry and to foster a social and political climate that is supportive of high-quality survey research. (*See also* AAPOR; NCPP.)

CATI Computer assisted telephone interviewing. Telephone surveys in which the interviewer uses a computerized form of the questionnaire, as is done with CAPI.

Census Gathering data from all elements in a population, rather than just from a sample of elements as in a survey or poll. A census is sometimes called an enumeration.

Closed-end question A poll question that provides all respondents with a predetermined set of response alternatives from which to choose, rather than allow them to answer in their own language. This can be done explicitly by asking a question and providing answers such as "very likely," "somewhat likely," "somewhat unlikely," or "very unlikely" or implicitly by phrasing the question so that the answers are either "yes" or "no." The set of response alternatives must be both mutually exclusive and exhaustive. (*See also* Open-end questions.)

Confidence interval In a poll that uses a probability sample, the range of variation around a poll finding within which the poll is likely to be an accurate reflection of the population value. Confidence intervals are calculated by taking the poll's margin of error and adding it to and subtracting it from the poll's findings. For example, a poll with a margin of error of ±4 percent that finds that 45 percent of the public supports candidate A has a confidence interval on this finding that ranges from 41 to 49 percent. The pollster is then very confident (typically 95 percent of the time) that if a census had been conducted, the "true" value of the proportion supporting candidate A would be in the 41 to 49 percent range. Confidence intervals cannot be calculated for polls that are based on nonprobability samples.

Confidence level A statement of the likelihood that a relationship observed in a sample is merely due to chance. This likelihood is traditionally expressed as the number of times in 100 samples that this relationship could occur, usually as 1/100 or 5/100 times.

Confidentiality A pledge by the pollster to respondents that their responses will never be associated publicly with their names or any other identifying information. Confidentiality is not the same as anonymity, since the pollster (or at least the interviewer) does know identifying information about the respondent and thus can and does link answers to particular respondents.

Context effect The potential consequence of asking a question within the "context" of other questions such that the effect is to have the answers biased by the context. For example, asking about overall presidential job-approval ratings after asking a series of questions about specific aspects of the president's job performance appears to lower responses to the overall rating, thereby producing a bias. Context effects also can occur within a question stem or within sets of response alternatives to a question.

Contingency question A question whose answer determines which question is asked next. For example, answering "Don't know" to a question about which candidate a respondent intends to vote for may lead to a question that asks which candidate the respondent is "leaning toward." The "leaning" question is not asked of those who offered the name of a specific candidate in the earlier question.

Core voters Respondents who indicate strong support for a candidate and are unlikely to waiver in their support. This is determined by a series of questions following the measure of candidate preference.

Cover letter A way to make early "legitimizing" contact with sampled persons so as to "warm them up" to a subsequent in-person or telephone contact by an interviewer. These letters are printed on the letterhead of the polling firm or the poll's sponsor and explain the nature of the poll, how the person was sampled, and information about confidentiality. Such letters have been found to increase response rates, thus lowering the chances of nonresponse error. (*See also* Advance contact.)

Coverage The extent to which a poll's sampling frame includes ("covers") everyone in its target population. For example, a telephone poll of voters that uses a telephone directory as its sampling frame will not include any voter with an unlisted number.

Coverage error If a poll's sampling frame excludes some members of the target population, then there is a chance that its findings will not accurately reflect the target population. The size of the coverage error will depend on both the relative size of the group "missing" from the population and the size of the difference in attitudes and preferences between the group that is covered and the group that is missed. If the covered and uncovered groups hold similar attitudes and preferences, then coverage error will be negligible regardless of the relative size of the missing part of the population. Unfortunately, pollsters rarely know much about the magnitude of the differences, and thus the size of the coverage error, especially if the missing part of the population is large.

CRAP Computerized response audience polling. An approach to "polling" in which a local news anchor records a set of poll questions. Advanced telecommunications equipment is then used to place a telephone call, play the set of recorded questions to someone who answers the telephone line, and record the answers that are given via the touch-tone pad on the respondent's telephone. These are totally unscientific polls because there is no way of confidently knowing who has been "interviewed." The attraction of CRAP for the media organizations that sponsor them appears to be their low cost and quick turnaround. (*See also* SLOP.)

Cross-sectional survey   A poll that interviews one group of sampled respondents at one point in time. Most polls are cross-sectional, as opposed to *panel surveys* in which the same people are interviewed more than once. Different cross-sectional polls can be combined to create *tracking polls* if they ask exactly the same questions.

Demographic question   A poll item that measures any of the so-called vital statistics of the respondents. Typically, these are either physiological (such as gender, age, or race) or experiential (such as education, income, or marital status).

Dependent variable   Symbolically represented by the letter "Y" in equations, the dependent variable is one that is predicted by, and may be caused by, another (independent) variable. In political polls, party affiliation (an independent variable that indicates whether respondents identify themselves as Democrats or Republicans) often predicts *candidate preference.* If candidate preference can be predicted by party affiliation, then the preference is thought to be "dependent" upon affiliation. Originally, these terms (dependent and independent) were associated with experimental research studies in which scientists controlled the levels of exposure that subjects received of an independent variable (such as dosages of a new drug in medical studies) and then observed the effect, if any, on the dependent variable (such as changes in health).

Designated respondent   The one person within a household who is systematically chosen to be that unit's respondent. Several techniques are used to make this choice. What they all have in common is that they provide an "arbitrary" approach to choosing this individual that does not give the interviewer the freedom to choose which person to interview or to ask the questions of the first person who answers the phone or opens the door or whoever is willing to be interviewed. These techniques are all designed to increase the likelihood that the sample will be demographically representative of the population. Lower-quality polls, including those that are conducted overnight, do not employ such techniques because they increase the costs and the time to complete the poll.

Double-barreled question   Any item that includes two separate concepts that should properly be asked as two different items. For example, "How would you rate the president's job performance on crime and the economy?" Answers to double-barreled items are virtually impossible to interpret since the pollster cannot know to which part of the item respondents meant their answers to apply.

Double negative A problem with the wording of a poll item caused by including two negatives in the same question. This makes it difficult for respondents to understand the question and answer it accurately, almost certainly contributing to the error in the data for the item. For example, asking respondents, "To what extent are you opposed to not allowing prayer in the public schools," is very confusing wording and places a great burden on the respondents to figure out what answer to give in order to reflect their own opinions about school prayer. Experienced pollsters find it easy to avoid creating items with double negatives.

800 poll An audience or reader call-in poll to a 1-800 telephone number that involves no cost to the caller. These are most often sponsored by a media organization that produces news, and they typically ask opinions about a single topic or question. A different telephone number is used by callers who "agree" and those who "disagree" with whatever issue position is being "surveyed." Such polls are totally unscientific because there is no way to know what target population is represented by those who choose to dial in. (*See also* 900 poll.)

Election night projections On the evening of a primary or general election, television broadcasts now routinely make projections of which candidate will win. Depending on the sophistication of the methods used to gather the information used in these projections, they can be extremely accurate. VNS (Voter News Service) is the organization created by a consortium of national television networks and the Associated Press to gather the information and provide these projections for major elections. VNS uses exit-poll data, returns from key precincts, and past voting patterns to formulate its projections. Research shows that a majority of the public says they find "early projections" objectionable, including accurate ones. (*See also* Exit poll; VNS.)

Elements Members of a population or a sample. A sample consists of the selected elements from the population. In a poll, the respondent is the sampled person from whom data are gathered. In most election polls, a household is the unit that is sampled first, and then within the household one person is selected to be the respondent (element).

Epsem sample A probability sample in which each element has an equal chance of being sampled, thus the name "Equal Probability of Selection Method." (*See also* Probability sample.)

Exhaustive A characteristic of an item's set of response alternatives that means that all possible answers to the question must fit into one of the closed-end response choices or one of the code categories for an open-end question. (*See also* Mutually exclusive.)

Exit polls Face-to-face polling of voters leaving their voting places on primary or general election day. As conducted by the network-sponsored election research firm VNS, sampled voters are handed a two-page questionnaire, printed back-to-back, on a clipboard. When they have completed the questionnaire, respondents place it into a cardboard "ballot box." Data are gathered in a relatively small number of sampled precincts within the geopolitical area being surveyed. Interviewers try to use a selection rule to select every nth voter exiting the voting place for an interview. Exit polls gather data that are used to help make election night projections of winners and to analyze voting patterns in the electorate. Many people hold the view that "early projections of winners" based on exit polls have affected past election outcomes, although no definitive evidence is available to support that contention. (*See also* Election night projections.)

Face-to-face interviewing Polling in which a human interviewer administers the questionnaire in person to the respondent. Traditionally, this has been done by having the interviewer travel to a potential respondent's home, knock on the door, and ask to come inside to conduct the interview. This mode of data collection is not now often used because of its costs and other practical disadvantages compared to telephone interviewing. Face-to-face interviews allow for longer and more complicated questionnaires compared to other modes of interviewing.

Favorability ratings A type of poll item that measures whether or not a respondent approves of (is favorable to) or disapproves of (is unfavorable to) an incumbent's performance in office or a candidate's professed policies. The favorability score that is calculated from these data is the difference between the percentage of those sampled who are "favorable" and the percentage who are "unfavorable." For example, if 40 percent of the electorate held a favorable view of the president, whereas 45 percent held an unfavorable view (with 15 percent undecided), the president's Favorability Rating would be slightly "negative" ($40\% - 45\% = -5\%$). (*See also* Approval ratings.)

Field period The time that elapses between the start and finish of data collection. Most polls conducted for the news media have very short field periods, ranging from a few hours (as in surveys conducted on the evening of a televised debate) to the more common two or three days. Most polls conducted for candidates also have short field periods because of the need to get data back quickly. Academic surveys of political issues generally use much longer field periods, often a month or more. A general rule is that the shorter the field period, the higher the nonresponse, and thus the greater the chance for serious nonresponse error.

Focus group A moderated small-group discussion, generally with eight to ten participants. A moderator takes the group through a prearranged discussion agenda in a way that tries to simulate a "real world" group discussion as much as possible, without the moderator's own opinions biasing the discussion. Unlike polls with scientific sampling designs, information gathered from focus groups has no scientific representativeness. But a focus group can provide richer and more detailed feedback on issues such as reactions to certain types of political advertising than is typically gathered by way of a structured poll questionnaire.

Frequency distribution A table or set of numbers that represent the answers given by respondents to one question in a poll. The answers are aggregated (grouped) for each possible response alternative across all possible responses. This aggregation can be done as simple counts (absolute frequencies) or as percentages (relative frequencies). For example, the following aggregation adds to 100 percent and is a distribution of relative frequencies to a question that uses a "strongly approve" to "strongly disapprove" response scale: 13 percent strongly approve, 27 percent approve, 42 percent disapprove, 10 percent strongly disapprove, 8 percent are uncertain. (*See also* Marginals.)

FRUGing Fund raising under the guise of legitimate polling. An unscrupulous and unethical practice that tricks people into thinking they are being interviewed for a real poll when instead they are being set up for an eventual fund-raising pitch. In a mail solicitation, the respondent may see a "questionnaire" composed of leading questions about an issue that concludes with a request for help by making a financial contribution. In a telephone survey, the pitch for money may come some time after the "polling" is completed, and the "respondents" whose answers suggest that they would make likely donors may not even make the connection between the two telephone calls. (*See also* SUGing.)

Gender gap A term created by some political analysts in the 1980s and embraced by the news media to refer to the consistent differences observed between women and men in the candidates they favor and their opinions on various policy issues. In the 1992 general election, for example, there was a statistically significant and sizable difference in voting behavior by men and women that led to a "gender gap." Women's votes divided 46 percent for Clinton, 37 percent for Bush, and 17 percent for Perot, compared to men who voted 41 percent for Clinton, 38 percent for Bush and 21 percent for Perot. Thus there was

a gender gap of 5 percentage points of women favoring the Democratic candidate.

Horserace journalism The tendency of reporters, editors, and producers to
focus election coverage predominantly on which candidate is ahead or
behind in the race or will be the likely victor. Sometimes this emphasis seems to preclude reporting news related to policy issues that
might better educate the electorate and thus advance public discourse
in ways that are thought to help democracy. Horserace journalism also
includes the proclivity of many journalists to cover an election campaign as a contest or "game," often using the language and metaphors
of sports reporters to characterize the winning and losing strategies
used by the respective candidates' campaign teams. Criticism of this
approach notwithstanding, which candidate will win "the horserace" is
a major news story. (*See also* Trial-heat question.)

Independent variable Symbolically represented by the letter "X" in equations, the independent variable is one that predicts, and may cause,
another (dependent) variable. In the analysis of election polls, demographic and background variables such as gender, age, region of the
country, party affiliation, and education often serve as independent
variables. They are used to compare, and thus help understand, responses to dependent variables such as candidate preference and political attitude questions. (*See also* Dependent variable.)

Informed consent A standard of ethics practiced by scrupulous pollsters
that first informs all respondents about their rights and about any potential harm that may come from their voluntary participation in a
poll. Pollsters seek the consent of respondents to participate in the
poll before they ask questions. Informed consent can be accomplished
through a variety of wordings of a poll's introduction. Often the process is implicit and leads to informal consent on the part of the respondent, instead of using explicit language to gain the respondent's
formal consent.

Insert polls Pages "inserted" in a magazine or newspaper containing questions for a poll. Readers self-select themselves as respondents by tear-
ing out the pages, answering the questions, and then mailing or faxing
them to the publication. Insert polls have no control over sampling
and thus have little value as accurate measures of anything. Nevertheless, they can serve as vehicles for a newspaper or magazine to "engage" its readers by "courting" their opinions.

Intercept polls/samples Face-to-face surveying that stops (or intercepts)
respondents in public areas such as shopping malls, downtown street
corners, airports, or the like and asks them to complete a poll or other

type of research task. Used mostly for market research, intercept surveys use nonprobability samples and suffer from not knowing with any confidence what target population is represented by the sample.

Introductory spiel The words read by an interviewer at the start of contact with a potential respondent. The purpose of the spiel is to structure the information that the interviewer conveys in order to increase the chance that the sampled respondent will agree to participate. An introductory spiel typically conveys information about the nature and purpose of the poll, the name of the poll's sponsor, the name of the organization conducting the poll, how the person was sampled, and the confidentiality (if any) of participation. All this can be accomplished in a few skillfully worded sentences that the interviewer can and should supplement if questioned by the respondent.

Leaners Persons who say that they have not yet made a final decision about the candidate they will vote for, but who are asked which candidate they are leaning toward. In analyzing the data from a preelection poll, most pollsters will "discount" the reported preferences of leaners when doing the calculations that aim to project the election outcome, by according them less weight than those from respondents with a firm candidate preference. (*See also* Core voters.)

Likelihood of voting The probability that a given respondent will actually vote in a forthcoming election. Pollsters have developed their own "secret formulas" to measure voting likelihood because a valid method provides the pollster (and the clients) a competitive advantage over another pollster with less valid methods to assess likelihood. Likelihood of voting is usually measured through an index composed of a number of questions. These usually include registration status, whether or not a person voted in the last similar election, the respondent's own estimate of his or her intention to vote, and party affiliation. Persons not registered to vote in a given election have a zero likelihood of voting, and they will not be eligible for selection to participate in most election polls. (*See also* Probable electorate.)

Likely voter A poll respondent who has provided answers that cause the pollster to conclude that the person probably will, in fact, vote in the upcoming election. The criteria that many pollsters use to classify a respondent as "likely" shift as the election nears. The ability of pollsters to differentiate likely voters from unlikely voters with accuracy is an important part of the art and science of election polling. (*See also* Probable electorate.)

Longitudinal studies A form of polling in which the same questions are administered over time so changes in attitudes or other measures can be assessed. When the same respondents are interviewed at more than one point in time, this is called a *panel study*. Each time interviews are conducted is called a *wave;* thus, a longitudinal survey has at least two waves of data collection. The passage of time between waves may be fixed (e.g., once each month) or variable (e.g., before election primaries or before the conventions). Another form of longitudinal study involves the same questions being asked of separate samples. These are known as *repeated cross-sections*. Both types of longitudinal designs are used to measure change over time.

Mail survey A poll that sends a questionnaire to a household or an individual via the mail. Thus the questionnaire is self-administered without the participation of an interviewer. Nowadays, "mail" surveys include those disseminated via fax and/or the Internet (e-mail). Insert surveys are a form of mail surveying as the respondents complete the questionnaire at a time of their choosing and "mail" the questionnaire back. Mail surveys have the advantage of relatively low cost, and they allow respondents to take as much time to think about their answers as they choose. Their disadvantages are the time they take to do well and the uncontrolled setting in which the questionnaire is actually completed. Mail surveys are rarely used by the news media for election polling because they take so long to conduct well, typically a month or longer to achieve an acceptable response rate.

Marginals This term sometimes refers to the frequency distribution for a single variable. It also applies to the frequency counts or percentages that can be summed down each column and across each row of the table that contains the cross-tabulation of two poll questions. For example, the answers to an attitudinal question given by men and women are called the "marginals" because they appear at the margins of the table. (*See also* Frequency distribution.)

Margin of error More properly termed the margin of "sampling" error, this is a statistical measure that is only meaningful when a probability sample is used. It is a measure of variation, or uncertainty, associated with any finding of a poll, and is due to the fact that a poll is not a census. Because not everyone in the target population is measured, there is a chance (a nonzero probability) that the poll findings are in error, even to a very small extent, simply because a sample was selected. With a probability sample, formulas can be used to calculate the size of this error within a known degree of confidence—typically the 95 percent level of confidence. Thus a sample of 1,100 respondents has a margin of error of approximately ±3 percent, indicating that 19 times out of 20 the population or "true" value lies within the sample estimate ±3 percentage points. The margin of error is often reported by the news media, whereas the fact that there are other likely sources of error in any poll, such as low response rates or elements of the questionnaire, is not. (*See also* Confidence interval.)

Measurement error Possible sources of bias and variance in poll findings due to the questionnaire (its wording and/or ordering), the interviewers' behavior (purposeful or unintended), the respondent (purposeful or unintended) and the mode (face-to-face, telephone, or mail). Serious pollsters try to use methods that are likely to reduce these potential causes of error. No matter what is done, however, the likelihood remains that some small level of measurement error will exist. If resources allow, a pollster can try to estimate the size of some potential sources of measurement error—by gathering extra data or doing extra analyses—and then make adjustments (corrections) to the data before reporting them.

Media polls Election surveys sponsored (and possibly conducted) by news organizations. Most media election polls gather data about both candidate preferences and political attitudes. Critics of the media's use of the data gathered via these polls believe that they contribute to the media's fascination with the "horserace." Media organizations sponsor polls to provide themselves with a competitive news advantage and to have access to information that has been gathered explicitly for the organization's own news purposes.

Methods box A "sidebar" that is often printed in a newspaper or magazine to accompany an article reporting poll results. The methods box provides the reader with information about how the poll was conducted, typically including the mode of data collection, the target population that was sampled, the sample size, the dates of data collection, information about the margin of sampling error, and whether any statistical weighting adjustments were made after the data were gathered.

Mutually exclusive An attribute of a set of response alternatives to closed-end poll items or the code categories for any open-ended response that makes it logically impossible for a respondent's answer to be coded into more than one of the response choices.

NCPP The National Council of Public Polls. An umbrella organization of companies that conduct surveys and polls. Founded in 1969, NCPP is interested in high-quality public opinion polling. It publishes a set of disclosure standards for organizations that produce polls for public consumption. (*See also* AAPOR; CASRO.)

900 poll An audience or reader call-in poll to a 1-900 telephone number for which the caller has to pay a charge, sometimes a very expensive one. These are most often sponsored by a media organization that produces entertainment programming, and they typically ask opinions about a single topic or question. Otherwise, they are similar in method to 800 polls and are just as limited in terms of known accuracy. (*See also* 800 poll.)

Noncontacts A sampled household or person who is never contacted by the poll. In face-to-face and telephone surveys, this results from such factors as addresses or telephone numbers that do not reach the correct household/person or sampled people never being at home or being unable to talk to the interviewer at the times interviewers try to make contact. In mail surveys, this results from incorrect mailing addresses. Noncontacts are a source of nonresponse, and they can be reduced by doing several callbacks. Noncontacts are more prevalent when trying to reach males and adults under the age of thirty.

Nondirective probing A type of behavior that well-trained interviewers use in order to avoid biasing responses to open-end poll items. Nondirective probing allows interviewers to remain neutral while they encourage respondents to answer a question more fully. Nondirective probing strives to eliminate interviewer-related error that could distort (bias) the answers that respondents provide.

Nonprobability sample Any of several different sampling schemes (such as quota, snowball, or convenience designs) in which the elements in the "sampling frame" do not have both a known and a nonzero probability of selection. Thus it is impossible to calculate the size of the poll's margin of sampling error with a nonprobability sample. Of note, this statistical fact does not stop some pollsters from calculating sampling error with a nonprobability sample—it simply makes their calculations meaningless. Nonprobability samples are useful in the early stages of research or when a pollster needs to gain an "impression" of the preferences and attitudes of a target population but does not need to be very confident about how well the poll generalizes to the target population.

Nonresponse Present in virtually all polls, nonresponse occurs whenever no data are gathered from a sampled element (person or household). The primary sources of nonresponse are noncontacts and refusals. Other minor sources are language or a respondent's physical and mental difficulties. Nonresponse is especially problematic in polls with short field periods because the limited amount of time precludes the use of multiple callbacks to reduce noncontacts and lowers the efficiency of trying to convert initial refusals. It is likely that most media polls achieve response rate of less than 50 percent (less than half those sampled are actually interviewed), due in part to their relatively short field periods.

Nonresponse error If the group of sampled persons in a poll who never are interviewed differ in meaningful ways in their preferences and attitudes from those who are interviewed, a poll will contain nonresponse error. The size of this error is related to the level of nonresponse and to the magnitude of the difference between the preferences or attitudes of those who responded and those who did not. Nonresponse error probably is the single most serious cause of inaccuracy in otherwise good-quality polls—ones that use reasonable questionnaires and good interviewing techniques.

Nonsampling error A term devised to contrast all sources of survey error (bias and variance) other than those related to sampling error. The sources of nonsampling error include coverage error, nonresponse error, and measurement error. Pollsters can utilize many methodological techniques either to try to reduce the possible size of these errors or to measure their size if they cannot be eliminated or reduced.

Open-end questions Poll questions that allow respondents to answer in their own words rather than limiting the range of responses to a predetermined set of alternatives. These answers are recorded "verbatim." Open-end answers, while providing information that can be much richer, more detailed, and more valid than closed-end data, have a very serious disadvantage for most polls in that they require laborious coding into meaningful categories before they can be analyzed. Sometimes these questions are used in media polls to provide "juicy quotes" to humanize a numerical finding from a closed-end item. (*See also* Closed-end question; Verbatim responses.)

Opinion questions Closed-end poll questions that measure more transitory or specific "beliefs" about current political or public policy issues. Although some people use the terms "opinion" and "attitude" interchangeably, most social scientists contrast opinions with measures of attitudes, more general and fundamental views. Often posed as a statement to which a respondent is asked to agree or disagree, e.g., "Do you oppose or favor the new bill in the state legislature that would make it legal for a woman to get an abortion for any reason of her choice? Do you strongly oppose it, oppose it, favor it, or strongly favor it?"

Order effects The possible biasing effect that can result from the order (or "context") in which a poll item is asked of respondents. Research has shown conclusively that some questions are answered differently depending on what has been asked before them in the poll. Pollsters try to eliminate order effects by doing a considerable amount of pretesting of their questionnaires using different orders. Or they can randomize the order of certain questions and then take different response patterns to these items into account at the time the data are being analyzed. As both these approaches add to the cost of polling, they are not often used to their full potential for making polls more accurate. (*See also* Context effect.)

Panel studies A survey design in which the same set of respondents are interviewed at more than one point in time. When they are asked the same questions, this provides an excellent way to measure the full extent of change among the sampled respondents. (*See also* Longitudinal surveys.)

PAPI Paper-and-pencil-interviewing. Until the microcomputer revolution of the 1980s, virtually all polling was done using a questionnaire printed on paper with answers recorded on the pages with a pencil. Pencils are preferred over pens because they make it easier for interviewers to change what they record. PAPI is rarely used in telephone polls nowadays, although it is still needed when a polling firm's computer system "crashes" or when the need to conduct a poll arises so quickly that the software programming required to computerize the questionnaire would take too long. Of note, research has found that, on average, a questionnaire with PAPI takes 10 to 20 percent less time than its computerized version for interviewers to administer because PAPI affords the interviewer more control over pacing. (*See also* CAPI.)

Poll Literally, a counting of heads. When used to refer to a type of social research, a poll is a form of sample surveying that arose in the early 1800s as a way of "canvassing" the voting preferences of easily accessible subsets of the electorate (in bars, trains, or at rallies) in order to predict the likely election winner. These early "straw polls" used unscientific convenience samples to capture public opinion, which was then reported in newspaper stories. Nowadays, the term "poll" typically is used to represent any political sample survey of the electorate conducted by the media, politicians, or political interest groups that aims for a relatively quick and somewhat cursory tally of the public's political opinions and preferences. Academic survey groups occasionally conduct studies that they call "polls," but they usually have longer field periods (thus higher response rates), use more thoroughly pretested questionnaires, and release their findings without the "deadline" pressures of most other pollsters.

Pollster A person who conducts polls, typically for paying clients.

Population The group that a sample is supposed to represent. In election polls, the population may be all adults within a geopolitical unit, such as a precinct or city; all registered adults; or all likely voters. For many practical reasons, a poll's population is almost never entirely included in its sampling frame, the list of all elements in the population. To the extent that the sampling frame does not include all members of the population, the sample may lead to considerable coverage error.

Precision The extent to which a poll finding, such as the percentage of likely voters who will support candidate X, is an accurate measure of the "true" value in the population. The difference between the estimate derived from the sample and the population value may be due to a number of factors. Polls that use probability samples can calculate the size of the poll's imprecision that is due to sampling error. The size of the imprecision caused by potential nonsampling errors, such as those associated with noncoverage, nonresponse, or measurement problems, cannot be calculated as readily or as confidently (*see* Confidence interval).

Preelection polls Any poll that takes place before an election. Usually this means before a general election but after a primary; sometimes the term refers to a preprimary poll. Traditionally, the main purpose of these polls is to predict the winner of the election. The closer the poll is taken to Election Day, the more likely the poll will be accurate, all other considerations being equal. The past two decades have witnessed considerable criticism of the media's use of preelection polls as part of so-called horserace journalism.

Preprimary polls Polls conducted prior to a primary but close enough to primary election day to be a reasonable measure of the voting preferences of those who will turn out for the primary. Of note, there is an unfortunate paradox associated with preprimary polls, especially those conducted by or for the news media. The primary electorate is often more volatile in its preferences because many people have limited information about the candidates early in the campaign process, and it is also more difficult to estimate turnout in primaries than in a general election. At the same time, fewer resources are typically committed to preprimary polls than to preelection polls, thus making them even less likely to be accurate.

Presidential approval A type of poll question that was first asked by pollsters in the 1940s, and thus one of the longest-running time series of poll data available. The item asks respondents to indicate the extent to which they approve or disapprove of the manner in which the current president is handling the "job" of being the nation's chief executive.

(*See also* Favorability ratings.)

Pretest The testing of a questionnaire (or other part of a poll, such as its introductory spiel) before regular data collection actually begins. The purpose of a pretest is to improve the way the questionnaire works, including the wording of its items, the order of items within the questionnaire, and the length of the interview. Traditionally this has been done by conducting "practice interviews" with a small number of respondents (twenty to twenty-five) who are not necessarily randomly sampled. In the past decade, new approaches to pretesting have included "cognitive testing," which gathers in-depth information from a few respondents about such factors as what they think the poll's questions mean or what range of answers seem appropriate to them.

Prior restraint The ability of a government to control the release of certain types of news by a country's press. As it relates to election coverage, many democratic nations have laws that limit the timing of the media's release of news derived from preelection polls. The First Amendment to the U.S. Constitution prohibits the nation's federal, state, and local governments from engaging in prior restraint.

Probability sample Any of several different sampling approaches that share two attributes: each element in the sampling frame (population) has a known probability of being selected, and each element in the sampling frame has a nonzero probability of being selected. The great benefit of using a probability sample is that it allows the pollster to calculate the size of the poll's sampling error. Types of probability samples include simple random sampling, systematic sampling, stratified sampling, and cluster sampling. There are at least two commonly held misconceptions are about probability samples: (1) not all elements must have an equal chance of selection, and (2) some elements may have a 100 percent (that is, a certain) chance of selection.

Probable electorate The group of persons who are thought to be "likely voters," and thus are the part of the population that will determine the outcome of an election by their voting behavior. (*See also* Likely voter.)

Pseudo polls Any of several misguided or unscrupulous techniques that try to appear to be legitimate polls but are not. The primary purpose of these techniques, which often are conducted by political candidates or political interests groups, is to accomplish fund raising under the guise of polling or to convey partisan propaganda under the guise of polling. Innocent respondents are thus duped into believing that the "pollster" is sincerely interested in gathering their opinions. These pseudo polls are conducted both via telephone and through the mail. (*See also* FRUGing; Push polls; SUGing.)

Psychographic question A type of personal data gathered in some election polls that measures a variety of respondents' "personality" or lifestyle attributes. Such a question is linked to marketing research and is mostly used in private polls to devise political advertising or to determine how best to appeal to different segments of the electorate ("market").

Public opinion As it relates to election polling, public opinion includes the attitudes, preferences, and beliefs of "the public" (typically defined as adults in a society) about a host of political and public policy issues. Critics of election polling contend that polls reduce public opinion to mere numbers and thereby distort what the public really believes or prefers on political topics. Other pollsters, such as social critic Daniel Yankelovich, contend that traditional polling as it is used by the news media often fails to distinguish the complexity of opinions and "judgments" held by the public and thereby does not serve democratic discourse very well.

Push polls A method of pseudo polling in which political propaganda is disseminated to naive respondents who have been tricked into believing they have been sampled for a poll that is sincerely interested in their opinions. Instead, the push poll's real purpose is to expose respondents to information, conveyed in the poll "questions," that favors a specific candidate or political view in order to influence how they will vote in an election.

Questionnaire The entire set of items used to gather data in a mail survey or in a poll interview. The questionnaire begins after the poll's introductory spiel and its respondent selection method, if one is used. Election polls generally begin with questions that measure political attitudes, then measure voting intentions, and end with items on the respondents' demographic characteristics.

Question stem The part of a poll item that sets forth the substance or focus of the question being asked. The question stem does not include the response alternatives. A question stem may be balanced or unbalanced.

Random Something that happens without purposeful choice. In random sampling, the selection of an element from a sampling frame is arbitrary (thus unpredictable) and done in such a way that every element has a fair chance (probability) of selection. Randomness provides the underpinnings for "representative" sampling in that it makes it highly probable that the chosen sample will accurately represent the target population.

Random assignment Not often used in election polling, this is a technique that randomly (arbitrarily) assigns different question wordings or orderings to different respondents who are interviewed in the same poll. By doing this, data are produced that the pollster can use to analyze cause-and-effect relationships to learn whether or not differences in the question wording, for example, cause changes in the answers that respondents give. Random assignment is a very powerful research technique because it provides a valid way to test hypotheses in an experimental way and thus explain why something has happened.

Random error One of the two components of the error in polls, also known as "variance" in statistical terms. Random error and systematic error (bias) make up total poll error. Unlike bias, which is a consistent distortion away from the "true" level of an attitude or preference in the target population, random error makes poll findings less precise by expanding the "uncertainty" around any finding. Sampling error is a primary source of random poll error. Other possible causes of random poll error include ambiguously worded questions, interviewing that varies in quality, and inattentive respondents. Random error reduces the confidence that a pollster has when interpreting a poll finding.

Random sampling Any method that selects poll respondents randomly (arbitrarily) and gives each possible respondent a fair chance of being selected. When used with a probability sampling design, random sampling provides the basis for calculating a poll's margin of sampling error. Without random sampling, it is meaningless to calculate the size of sampling error. There are many different ways that random sampling can be accomplished. Nowadays, computers are commonly used to create the randomization.

RDD Random-digit dialing. A form of random sampling in telephone surveys that is the predominant method of sampling for election polls because it avoids the coverage error that would likely result if sampling were done from telephone directories. RDD allows a pollster to sample people who live in households that do not publish or list their telephone numbers. An RDD procedure randomly creates the numbers that interviewers dial by choosing a three-digit prefix (exchange) that rings in the geopolitical area in which the poll is conducted and then randomly assigning digits to the prefix to create a seven-digit local telephone number. This local number may or may not reach a household, regardless of whether or not the number is listed or in current use. People with unlisted telephone numbers often are concerned that polls can reach them via this method, but nevertheless most choose to participate as respondents in good-quality polls.

Recontact An attempt to complete an interview with a sampled respondent who was previously unavailable. The purpose of recontacts, despite the expense they add to polls, is to increase response rates and thereby lessen the chances for serious nonresponse error. Without recontact attempts, most polls will interview a sample that is disproportionately composed of women and older adults and thus is unrepresentative of the population as a whole.

Refusal Any time a sampled respondent tells an interviewer that he or she will not participate in a poll. Refusals are a major source of nonresponse in polls and may lead to a serious level of error in a poll's findings. If time allows in a telephone poll, pollsters can have skilled interviewers call back initial refusals to try to convince them to participate (an attempt to "convert" them). Experience suggests that women and older adults are more likely than men and younger adults to refuse to participate in polls.

Refusal conversion An attempt to convince a sampled respondent who has previously refused to participate in an interview. Using skilled interviewers, this process typically succeeds in about three in ten cases. It is unclear whether or not this somewhat costly effort actually reduces nonresponse error, thereby improving the poll's accuracy. If it does not reduce nonresponse error, there is little cost/benefit advantage for a pollster to attempt refusal conversions. It is generally agreed among ethical pollsters that a respondent who explicitly has said, "Don't call me back," should not be the recipient of a refusal conversion callback.

Refusal rate The proportion of sampled persons who are contacted by an interviewer and refuse to participate in a poll. Refusal rates for many polls exceed 30 percent, that is, one-third or more of contacted respondents refuse to participate.

Representative sample The extent to which a sample matches the demographic, attitudinal, or other characteristics of a target population it is intended to represent. It is not always understood that random sampling does not, in itself, ensure that the resulting sample will be representative. This is because even with random samples, chance variation can lead to significantly under- or oversampled subgroups of the target population. Nevertheless, random sampling minimizes the chance of this happening. One way pollsters check on the representativeness of their samples is to match a sample's demographic characteristics to population statistics from a recent census.

Respondent burden A term that refers to the effort that a respondent must put in to complete an interview. This "burden" might be small or large depending on how long the questionnaire is, how difficult the questions are to answer, and whether or not the questions cause the respondent any emotional difficulty. All these factors contribute to the burden borne by the respondent. But the vast majority of polls do not cause any undue or unpleasant level of burden on participants.

Respondents The people selected to be interviewed for a poll. With most household-based sampling used by election polls, the household is the unit that is first sampled, then one person is selected from within the household to serve as the respondent. When there is only one eligible person in the household to interview, as is the case for people who live alone, the selection of the respondent is automatic. In households with two or more persons who fit the poll's "eligibility criteria," some form of within-unit selection is used to choose one of these persons as the designated respondent in that household. People who agree to serve as poll respondents should understand that their participation is entirely voluntary and that no harm will come to them regardless of whether or not they choose to participate.

Response alternatives The set of answers used in a closed-end item from which respondents are expected to choose the one that best fits their answer to the question. For example, "very likely, somewhat likely, somewhat unlikely, or very unlikely." When the respondent is presented with a set that does not include a "Don't know" or "Undecided" alternative, the alternatives are called a "forced choice" set because they force the respondent to choose one of the substantive responses. Sets of response alternatives may be balanced, if they include a true midpoint, or unbalanced.

Response rates Several different measures that reflect various aspects of the proportion of sampled persons who actually completed the questionnaire. No poll achieves a 100 percent response rate because there always are people who cannot be contacted during the field period (because they are sick or on vacation, for example) or who refuse to be interviewed. Response rates are affected by such factors as the length of the field period, the quality of the interviewing, and the topic of the poll. There is some disagreement among pollsters and other survey researchers over what is considered to be a "low" response rate. Those working for the federal government often consider rates below 90 percent to be low, compared to those in academic settings who generally regard rates below 70 percent as low. In contrast, many pollsters in the private sector think response rates are not low until they fall below the 40 to 50 percent level. What really matters from the standpoint of polling accuracy, however, is not what the response rate is, but whether the poll has nonresponse error. If it does not, then the poll's accuracy will not suffer because of its nonresponse. (*See also* Nonresponse error.)

Rolling averages A term that refers to the numerical findings of tracking polls, whereby small daily samples of respondents are summed across three-day periods. For example, estimates are calculated for the periods Monday-Tuesday-Wednesday, Tuesday-Wednesday-Thursday, Wednesday-Thursday-Friday, and so on. Then the response "averages" for each three-day set are compared to see if any change or trend in intentions or attitudes is present. The problem with looking for change in rolling averages is that chance variation due to sampling error can make it appear that something has changed when in fact it has not, especially when small sample sizes are involved.

Sample The group, or subset, of some larger population that is selected to participate in a poll. Depending on how the sample is chosen from the population, the pollster may be able to calculate the extent to which the information collected from the sample is likely to represent the population, as is the case with probability samples. Any group of people who are interviewed can be termed a sample, but that does not mean that anyone (including the pollster) necessarily knows what population they represent if a probability design is not used. Whenever a sample is "drawn" (chosen) in a way that precludes having confidence about what population it represents, then the resulting data are virtually useless as indicators of the intentions or opinions of anyone other than those who were sampled.

Sample design The method used to select a sample for a poll. A basic and critical distinction in sample designs is whether a probability or nonprobability design is used. With a probability design—one in which each element in the sampling frame has a known, nonzero probability of selection—the pollster can calculate the size of the poll's sampling error. No meaningful calculation of the size of sampling error can be done with nonprobability samples.

Sample precinct A sampling unit used in exit polling. Within each sample precinct, a random sample of voters are interviewed as they leave their voting places. The national exit poll that VNS will conduct for ABC, CBS, CNN, NBC and other news organizations on Election Day in November 1996 will be based on interviews taken in a total of about 300 sample precincts, chosen by stratified random sampling.

Sample size The number of elements, typically people, selected from a population. This may refer to the number of elements at the start of the poll or the number of interviews eventually obtained. The larger the sample size, the smaller the margin of sampling error, all other factors being equal.

Sampling error When using a probability sample, a pollster can employ statistical formulas to calculate the size of the "uncertainty" (variation) around a poll finding due to the fact that a sample was drawn rather than having an interview taken with every member of the population. For example, the percentage of the electorate who will support candidate X may vary from the proportion in the entire population merely because the estimate is based on a poll and not a census. Without a probability sample, it is meaningless to use the sampling error formulas, but that does not stop some pollsters from doing so, because their clients apparently do not know the difference. The size of a poll's sampling error is related to (1) the exact type of probability sample design that is used, (2) how similar or dissimilar (heterogeneous) the public's attitudes or intentions are on whatever is being measured, and (3) the sample size. There is only a minute relationship between the relative size of the sample and the size of the target population.

Sampling frame The "list" from which a sample is chosen that contains all of the elements in the population. If any part of the target population is missing from the sampling frame, there exists the possibility that the poll will have coverage error. This would be the case, for example, if a telephone poll used a telephone directory as its sampling frame. Most election polls utilize a random-digit dialing sampling frame, as these polls are conducted via telephone and want to sample people regardless of whether or not their telephone numbers are listed. This avoids the possibility of coverage error that might be associated with whether a number is listed or unlisted. (*See also* RDD.)

Sampling interval In systematic samples that select every nth element in a sampling frame, the sampling interval is the number of elements that are skipped between sampled elements. For example, if a systematic sample of 200 is drawn from a sampling frame of 2,000 registered voters, then the sampling interval is 10. (*See also* Systematic sample.)

Scientific sampling A systematic approach to selecting respondents from whom to gather data. Some would argue that only probability samples are "scientific." Others would suggest that nonprobability samples can be "scientific" as long as they are implemented in a systematic fashion such that others could reasonably repeat or replicate the sample.

Screening A process that sometimes is used at the end of a poll's introductory sequence—after the respondent has been told some basic information about the poll—in order to "screen in" eligible respondents and "screen out" ineligible ones. For example, shortly before Election Day, pollsters will try to screen in likely voters and screen out unlikely ones by asking a series of questions meant to differentiate those who will vote from those who will not. This allows the pollster to allocate most interviewing resources to gathering data from those who will vote rather than interview everyone. Screening sequences do not always work accurately when respondents are screened-in as eligible to be interviewed when in fact they are not, an "error of commission" is said to have occurred; when respondents are screened-out as ineligible when in fact they were, this is called an "error of omission."

Secret ballot A mode of gathering data in a poll that simulates the process used by voters when they actually cast their votes. Secret ballots are used in preelection polls very close to Election Day and in exit polls. In the latter case, the respondent who has just voted is typically handed a clipboard and pencil with a short questionnaire to complete. When the respondents finish, they fold the questionnaire and place it in a cardboard "ballot box" that the interviewer is holding.

Self-administered questionnaire Any questionnaire that a respondent fills out without the intervention of an interviewer. Traditionally, this has been done via a printed questionnaire that the respondent marks with a pencil or paper. Nowadays, this sometimes occurs with the respondent using a computer that presents the questionnaire, one item at a time, although this is not often used in election polls. Self-administered questionnaires typically are mailed to respondents, but may be distributed at meetings or printed in newspapers or magazines (*see* Insert polls).

Self-selected sample The result from any poll that allows respondents the "easy" opportunity to decide on their own whether or not to take the time to complete the questionnaire. Typically the accuracy of mail surveys has suffered because their response rates are low as a function of no interviewer involvement in trying to encourage people to respond at the time they receive the questionnaire. Self-selected samples are often biased because the motivations that lead certain people to decide to respond and others not to respond may be highly correlated with whatever topic is being measured by the poll. For example, a mail or call-in poll about attitudes toward gun control would most likely get responses from persons at the two extremes of the political spectrum on this issue. Because of self-selection, the pollster will not know how well the sample reflects the target population.

Simple random sample A method of choosing a sample from a population that merely bases the selection on a totally arbitrary (random) process. These selection criteria might involve using a series of random numbers to decide whom to include in a sample and whom to leave out. Of note, the use of random sampling neither assures that it is a probability sample or that it is a representative sample of the target population.

SLOP Self-selected listener opinion poll. These polls are frequently organized by broadcast media to assemble opinions by listeners or viewers. One significant problem is that there is no control over respondent selection because anyone can call in an opinion. (*See also* Call-in polls; CRAP; 800 poll; 900 poll.)

Snowball sample A nonprobability sampling technique that can be very useful when the pollster does not need to be certain about how well those who have been interviewed reflect the attitudes or intentions of a target population. Snowball sampling typically is used to find persons in "rare" subgroups in the population (e.g., persons who voted for Eugene McCarthy, John Anderson, and Ross Perot), by asking such people to "nominate" others like themselves for the pollster to contact, thus "snowballing" toward a final desired sample size.

Social desirability The tendency of people to want to present themselves in a "positive light" when someone else is asking them questions about their attitudes, experiences, or background. The tendency to over-report positive things about yourself and underreport negative things. This includes the tendency to give answers that a respondent perceives that an interviewer or pollster will consider "correct" answers. Social desirability can cause poll data to be biased; how much depends on how strong the effect is. Pollsters concerned about possible social desirability bias can add certain items to their questionnaires that will allow them to do analyses after the data have been gathered to estimate the size of the effects and try to correct for them before reporting the data.

Split-half design The use of a true experimental design within a questionnaire in order to assign different question wordings or orders to different subgroups of respondents at random. By using random assignment of the different questionnaire versions, the pollster can conduct powerful and valid tests of the cause-and-effect relationships between the versions (the independent variable) and the answers that respondents provide (the dependent variables). For example, one subgroup of respondents might be asked their candidate preferences without being reminded about the respective candidates' policy stances, while another group might be told this policy information first. Such a split-half design would allow the pollster to test whether the policy information caused any changes in the respondents' expressed preferences.

Standardized survey interviewing A form of asking poll questions in which interviewers are trained and monitored to assure that they read the items exactly as they are written in a pleasant but neutral voice and that they follow up open-end questions with nondirective probes in order to get respondents to give more complete answers in a way that does not bias the responses. The goal of standardized interviewing is more readily achieved in telephone polls than in face-to-face interviews because a supervisor should always be present during a phone poll. This is never practical in face-to-face polling.

Strata Subsets of a larger group, such as the categories that comprise a demographic characteristic. For example, the four categories, 18–29, 30–44, 45–59, and 60 and older, make up one set of strata for the age variable. Sampling can be assured of being more representative if a sampling frame can be ordered by strata that are relevant to the purpose of the sampling.

Stratified sample A form of probability sampling in which the sampling frame is ordered (or grouped) according to a relevant stratum or strata before the actual sample is selected. Stratified sampling can assure that the selection of respondents occurs in a way that accurately represents whatever characteristic(s) the frame is stratified upon. Thus, stratification decreases the poll's sampling error compared to what would happen with an otherwise random but unstratified sampling. For example, if a list of registered voters were grouped by gender, then sampling could be done in whatever proportion the pollster deemed appropriate for females and males. This would not necessarily happen if the list were unstratified and simple random sampling were performed.

Straw polls A form of gathering information about public opinion, in particular about voting intentions, that has been used in the United States since the early 1800s. Straw polls do not use any scientific approach to sample respondents and therefore their "findings" cannot be generalized with any confidence to represent the preferences of any group beyond those that were polled. Instead, they gather the opinions of people who are "conveniently" available in a variety of public and/or private places and gatherings. Their "data" may be collected orally or via a simple paper-and-pencil technique. They typically ask people to indicate for whom they intend to vote in an upcoming primary or election.

SUGing Selling under the guise of polling. An unethical form of "polling" conducted by some telemarketing firms. These firms have their "interviewers," who really are their sales staff, lead "respondents" into thinking that a real poll is being conducted, when instead it is simply the prelude to a sales pitch. The practice persists because of the assumption that the sales pitch will be more successful if the "interviewer" has had a chance to develop some rapport with the "respondent" before making the sales pitch. This correctly assumes that many people enjoy being asked to participate in a poll and that they will be more likely to stay on the phone if they think they are being polled than if they think they are being pitched. (*See also* FRUGing.)

Survey As opposed to a census, in which data are gathered from all members (elements) in a population, a survey gathers data from only a subset, or sample, of the population. The use of a sample is one defining characteristic of the research technique called a survey. Surveys can be (and are) conducted of a host of nonhuman and inanimate objects, such as sampling plants in a cornfield, fish in a pond, rocks on a mountainside, or cars on an assembly line. When they are well planned and implemented, surveys are an extremely cost-effective way to gather all types of information that is critical to accurate decision making in both the public and private sectors.

Systematic error Also called bias, this is a constant form of inaccuracy that can occur in research, such as election polling, and leads to a consistent distortion of findings away from the "truth." (*See also* Bias.)

Systematic sample A form of probability sampling in which respondents are chosen from a list in a repetitive, yet random, manner. This results by first calculating the size of the sampling interval that will be needed. For example, if a systematic sample of 500 is taken from a list of 10,000, then the interval will be 20. Second, a random number between 1 and 20 is chosen, for example "17." Thus, the sample will consist of the 17th person on the list, followed by every 20th person thereafter—the 37th, 57th, 77th, . . ., 9997th—to complete the sample of 500. This form of sampling can lead to a slight reduction in sampling error, compared to a simple random sample, because it forces sampling to take place evenly across the entire listing.

Target population The larger group of people, such as the "population" to which a pollster wants to be able to generalize a poll's findings. For election polls, the target population varies over the course of the election season as the size of the "probable" electorate changes. For pollsters to have confidence that their polls will accurately reflect the desired target population, they must use a sampling frame that "covers" the target population well, employ some form of probability sampling, and achieve acceptable response rates from those sampled. The target population of most media-sponsored national election polls is "likely voters (starting with adult citizens of the United States who are registered) among the noninstitutionalized population that lives in the forty-eight continental states, who speak English and have home telephone service."

Telephone households In 1996, approximately 95 percent of households in the United States had at least one telephone access line that rings in their home. Of those with telephone service at home, approximately one in six have more than one line. Those without telephone service, so-called nontelephone households, are disproportionately poor, non-whites, and live in rural areas of the South and Southwest. RDD sampling, the type used by many election polls, utilizes a sampling frame that theoretically includes all telephone households in the geopolitical area being polled.

Telephone surveys Surveys that sample people via their telephone number or have data gathered over the telephone. New telecommunications services, such as faxes and the Internet, are beginning to be used for survey and polls, but these are not properly termed telephone surveys, even though data are gathered via telephone lines.

Tracking polls A type of preelection surveying in which relatively small samples of respondents are interviewed each day for several days in a row. Often, each day's sample is independent (different) from the other days. The interviews gathered each day are then aggregated, typically over a three-day period, to look for trends in preferences and opinions. The serious problem of tracking polls is that their daily response rates are low, and daily fluctuations may be due merely to chance (sampling error). (*See also* Rolling averages.)

Trend analysis Using poll data to try to determine consistent and meaningful changes over some period of time, such as a week, month, or year. Trend analysis can be accomplished in one of three standard ways. It can be done with the data gathered by tracking polls, but only with great caution. It also can be done with data that come from panel studies, in which the same people are asked similar poll questions at different points during an election year. It can also be done with longitudinal studies in which different samples of people are asked the same questions at different times. Pollsters, reporters, and other political observers then try to link real-world events with the observed changes in order to explain why they are appear to be occurring. (*See also* Longitudinal surveys; Panel studies.)

Trial-heat question The item that asks respondents which candidate they prefer or how they intend to vote. Traditionally the most important question asked in an election poll, and usually asked very early within a questionnaire. This item is typically presented with some variation of the wording, "If the election were held today, ..." The responses to trial-heat items provide the data that drive horserace journalism.

True experiment A type of research design that randomly assigns respondents to at least two different conditions in order to produce data that allow for powerful and valid cause-and-effect analyses. (*See also* Split-half designs.)

Unbalanced question A question stem or set of response alternatives that are not "balanced." An unbalanced stem presents only one side of an issue rather than all sides. This is generally thought to bias responses to the item. An unbalanced set of response alternatives is simply one that is not symmetrical and therefore does not contain a true mid-point. Unbalanced response alternatives do not necessarily contribute to poll error.

Undecideds Those respondents who report in a trial-heat item that they have not yet made up their minds about which candidate they will vote for. The proportion of respondents who say they are undecided decreases the closer the poll is taken to Election Day. Pollsters often ask "undecideds" additional questions to determine toward which candidate they are "leaning."

Underdog effect A "sympathy" effect that apparently causes some voters who otherwise might be expected to vote for one candidate to support another candidate who preelection polls predict will lose the election. As with the bandwagon effect, definitive research on the underdog effect is very difficult to conduct and, therefore, not much is known with certainty about the effect. (*See also* Bandwagon effect.)

Uniform poll closings The legislative proposal that voting in person at polling places across the United States should take place during the same hours all across the country. This means that polls would close at the same moment, regardless of which time zone(s) the state falls within. The motivation for such a major procedural change is to keep the news media from making "early projections" based on eastern states whose polling places have closed several hours before voting is completed in western states. There are two groups of supporters for this change. One consists of critics who assume that "early projections" affect voting in western states. The other consists of media organizations who realize that this may be the only practical solution to the complaints that critics make. Despite what many politicians, journalists, and others in the public believe, however, no definitive research has ever demonstrated the size and direction of the effect of early election night projections on voter turnout or candidate preference.

Unit A sampling term that refers to the entity within which a respondent is selected to be interviewed. In election polls this is almost always a household or a home. In an RDD design, random sampling occurs first at the household unit level, before an individual within the housing unit is selected. In an exit poll, the first unit selected is a precinct, usually followed by a systematic sample of people who voted there.

Unlisted household A telephone household that pays its local telephone company a small monthly service fee to avoid having its telephone number given out by directory assistance. Unlisted numbers also are not published in local telephone directories, but unpublished numbers are not all "unlisted" with the local directory assistance. Research has found that unlisted telephone households are most likely to be found among African Americans, Hispanics, and several other minorities; families with lower socioeconomic status; in urban areas; and among those who live in some western states. Thus, any poll that uses a telephone directory as its sampling frame and asks about opinions or preferences that correlate with any of these demographic factors runs the risk of serious coverage error.

Variable As it relates to election polls, a *variable* is a question that is used to gather data from respondents. It is termed a variable because it is assumed that respondents' answers will vary from person to person, that is, they will not all be the same. If there were no variation in the answers, the measure instead would be a *constant*. Then there would be no need to ask the question because everyone's answer would always be known.

Verbatim responses The exact words used by a respondent to answer an open-end poll item. In self-administered polls, respondents write down their answers in their own words. In polls that use interviewers, the interviewer is expected to record the answer in the respondent's own words without summarizing them. This may require an interviewer to ask a respondent to slow down his or her speaking rate or to repeat part of the answer to a question so the interviewer can record information legibly.

VNS Voter News Service. The company that was formed in 1993 by combining the former Voter Research & Surveys and the News Election Service. The primary purpose of VNS is to gather election statistics, including exit-poll data, to support the election analysis of its media sponsors: ABC, CBS, CNN, NBC, and the Associated Press. This consortium of sponsors all receive the same data but analyze and report it separately. This joint approach saves these organizations several millions of dollars in data collection compared to what they would spend if each gathered the information separately.

Volatility The uncertainty associated with whether poll respondents will go to vote on Election Day as well as whether or not they will change their candidate preferences when they do. This kind of volatility has been growing in the American electorate, and it makes the prediction of election outcomes from preelection polls risky. Careful pollsters gather data within their polls to assess how volatile the electorate appears to be and then take this into consideration when they make their preelection predictions.

Voluntary participation A professional standard that is subscribed to and deployed by all ethical polling firms. It provides that all poll respondents are voluntary participants and that the firm and its employees will do nothing to coerce someone into participating. Thus, interviewers should always be trained to make it clear to any concerned respondent that their participation is voluntary and that no harm will come to them if they choose not to participate.

Vote-by-mail A relatively new approach to conducting elections in some states and local municipalities. In January 1996, for example, Oregon elected its new U.S. senator entirely by mail. Every registered voter received the information describing the candidates and a ballot that had to be mailed back to the county office by a set date. This approach to voting is creating new challenges to those who would otherwise be conducting election polls to measure voting behavior, either before Election Day or as an "exit poll," because voting takes place over time and there are no voting places at which to interview exiting voters.

Weighting Statistical adjustments to poll data that are conducted before they are analyzed. Weighting is used to adjust for respondents' unequal probabilities of selection in probability samples. It is also used by some pollsters to try to adjust for nonresponse in a final sample whose demographic characteristics do not match those of the target population very well. Sometimes, weighting is used to count the answers of certain respondents more heavily than others, such as when formulating the prediction of an election outcome from preelection poll data. In such a case, a pollster attaches greater weight to the answers of those respondents who are most likely to vote, compared to the answers of those whose likelihood of voting is less certain.

Index